THE
D·E·E·D·S
BOOK

By Attorney Mary Randolph

Illustrations by Mari Stein

NOLO PRESS • 950 PARKER STREET • BERKELEY • CA • 94710

IMPORTANT

Nolo Press is committed to keeping its books up-to-date. Each new printing, whether or not it is called a new edition, has been completely revised to reflect the latest law changes. This book was printed and updated on the last date indicated below. Before you rely on information in it, you might wish to call Nolo Press (415) 549-1976 to check whether a later printing or edition has been issued.

PRINTING HISTORY

New "Printing" means there have been some minor changes, but usually not enough so that people will need to trade in or discard an earlier printing of the same edition. Obviously, this is a judgment call and any change, no matter how minor, might affect you.

New "Edition" means one or more major, or a number of minor, law changes since the previous edition.

FIRST EDITION	June 1987

Book Design and Layout	JACKIE CLARK
	AMY IHARA
	KEIJA KIMURA
Cover Design	TONI IHARA
Production	STEPHANIE HAROLDE
Illustrations	MARI STEIN
Contributing Editor	IRA SERKES
Printing	DELTA LITHOGRAPH

ISBN 0-87337-040-6
Library of Congress Catalog Card. No.: 87-61275
Copyright © 1987 by Mary Randolph

ACKNOWLEDGEMENTS

My first thanks must go to Jake Warner and Steve Elias, who let themselves be talked into giving me a job at Nolo. When it comes to this book, it's trite but true: I couldn't have done it without them.

Sincere thanks also go to Jackie Clark, Keija Kimura, Amy Ihara, and Toni Ihara, who patiently designed the book and wrestled with the computers until it came out right, and to Mari Stein for her wonderful drawings.

But everyone at Nolo has a hand in this book in some way. So thank you, Stephanie Harolde, John O'Donnell, Claudia Goodman-Hough, Jack Devaney, Renee Rivera, Carol Pladsen, Kate Thill, Julie Christianson, Alison Towle, Barbara Hodovan, Ann Heron, David Cole and Susan Quinn.

Real estate experts Hayden Curry, Ira Serkes and George Devine and financial expert Malcolm Roberts provided help along the way and commented helpfully on the manuscript.

And thanks to my parents, who gave me genes for writing and law.

ABOUT THE AUTHOR

Nolo Press editor and author Mary Randolph received her J.D. from the University of California-Berkeley (Boalt Hall). Before that, she studied zoology at the University of Illinois, and no, she doesn't know quite how she ended up in law school, either.

Table of Contents

CHAPTER 7. RECORDING YOUR DEED

CHAPTER 8. WHEN YOU NEED AN EXPERT

GLOSSARY

C H A P T E R 1

How To Use This Book

You're reading this book because you have a task to accomplish: you want to find out how to transfer title to a piece of California real property. The mechanics of making this sort of change are usually not difficult. In many situations, the owners of the property need only fill out a straightforward deed form and file it at the county recorder's office.

This book shows you how to do that, but perhaps more importantly, it also alerts you to legal and practical considerations that have the potential to complicate your transfer. These include due-on-sale clauses in loans, federal gift taxes, and disclosure statements required by law. Don't be put off by their apparent complexity; it's very unlikely that more than a few of them will affect your transfer. Usually, the added inconvenience of taking care of them is slight.

A. WHAT THIS BOOK HELPS YOU DO

This book shows you how to transfer[1] or mortgage[2] title to almost any kind of California real property, including houses, land, farms, vacation homes, commercial buildings, and condominiums. Specifically, it provides the instructions and forms necessary to do the following:

• Transfer title to real property to one or more family members or friends;

• Put the title to your real property in joint tenancy form (commonly done for estate planning purposes so that property will automatically go to the surviving joint tenant without probate);

• Change the title to real property from a joint tenancy to another form, such as community property or tenancy in common;

• Place title to your real property in the names of additional owners, or remove one or more current co-owners from the deed (for example, if divorcing spouses want to convert jointly held property into the separate property of one spouse);

• Give up any legal claims of ownership you might have to certain real property;

• Execute a trust deed to secure payment of a loan; and

• Transfer real property to a living trust (for probate avoidance), or from a living or testamentary trust (trusts are explained in Chapter 4).

The potential tax and estate planning consequences of these property transfers are also covered briefly.

This book takes a functional approach to real property law. Instead of teaching you everything there is to know about the California law governing real property transfers (an impossible job), it gives you the basic information you need to make your transfer efficiently. Along the way, we alert you to

---

[1]For convenience, we refer to all kinds of ownership or title changes as transfers, even if the current owners just want to change the way they hold title to the property. For example, if joint owners of real property change the title from "Smith and Jones, as tenants in common" to "Smith and Jones, as joint tenants," it's as much a transfer, for our purposes, as if they sold the property to a third party. More on "title changes" later.

[2]Although the word "mortgage" is commonly used in California to describe the process of making real property security for a loan, the document actually used to do this is almost always a "deed of trust." Basically, a mortgage and a deed of trust amount to the same thing—you give property as security for a loan—but deeds of trust allow the lender a quicker and cheaper method of foreclosing if the borrower defaults on the loan. See Chapter 5.

circumstances that mean you need more detailed information or the special skills of a lawyer, real estate agent, or tax accountant.

Here are the steps you need to follow to use this book efficiently:

Step 1: Read Chapter 2 for an overview of the real property transfer process. It discusses many of the questions you should address before you make a transfer. For instance, you need to consider whether your transfer will be affected by local property tax reassessment rules, whether local transfer taxes will have to be paid, and whether or not the transfer will be subject to federal gift taxes. You should also pay attention to rules affecting existing deeds of trust or mortgages on the property—they may have to be paid off before you can transfer it. Finally, in certain circumstances, California law requires you to give a written disclosure statement to the prospective new owners, listing any known defects or problems with the property.

You may be tempted to skip or skim Chapter 2 and get on with the transfer. Please don't. What you learn about tax liability or the rules governing deeds of trust may convince you to change the way you make your transfer, or even convince you not to make it at all.

Step 2: In Chapter 3, we show you how to decide who must sign the deed to make the transfer valid. The general rule is simple—all owners must sign. In some cases, however, you may need the signature of someone whose name isn't on the current deed to the property.

Step 3: Your next step is Chapter 4, which discusses the ways in which the recipients of the property can take title to it (e.g., joint tenancy, tenancy in common, or community property).

Step 4: Next, you go to either Chapter 5 or Chapter 6 for specific instructions on how to prepare the deed you need. Chapter 5 is only for persons who want to execute a trust deed (to use property as security for a loan). Chapter 6 is where to go if you want to make any other kind of transfer covered by this book. Tear-out forms for all the deeds are included in the Appendix.

Step 5: The next step is to record your signed and notarized deed with the county recorder in the county where the property is located. Chapter 7 tells you how.

Step 6: Finally, if you have questions that this book doesn't answer, read Chapter 8 for some tips on how to get extra help from a lawyer, library, accountant or real estate agent.

B.   WHAT THE BOOK DOESN'T COVER

Now that we've discussed in some detail what this book can do, here are a few words about what it can't do.

1. Formal Transactions, Including Sales on the Open Market

This book does not cover real property transfers when a bank and a title or escrow company are involved. A typical "arm's length" real estate transfer (e.g., the sale of a house to a stranger) almost always involves property inspections, appraisals, title searches and insurance, and removal of contingencies included in the sales contract.[3] Lenders and title companies have their own procedures, and the whole bureaucracy is intent on seeing that you use, and pay for, its services. As a part of the process, the escrow holder[4] will fill out and record the deeds you need to transfer title to property. Even if you sell your own house without a broker, if the buyer gets a loan from a financial institution there is no practical way (or need) for you to intervene in this process and complete and record your own deed.

2. Out-of-State Property

This book only discusses California law and so only applies to California real property. If you want to transfer title to real property in another state, you will have to follow that state's rules for deeds and recording. Although state laws that govern real estate transfers follow the same general pattern, there can be important differences in the required deed language, in county recording procedures, or in rights of spouses. The point is that outside California you shouldn't use this book as more than a very general guide.

---

[3]For a step-by-step manual on how to sell residential property in California without a real estate broker, see *For Sale By Owner*, by George Devine (Nolo Press).

[4]An escrow holder is a neutral third party who—to greatly oversimplify—takes the buyer's money and the seller's deed and exchanges them. Usually a title or escrow company acts as an escrow holder.

3. Removing the Name of a Deceased Co-owner

The procedure to accomplish this depends on how title to the property was held (e.g., joint tenancy or community property). Sometimes only a simple affidavit must be recorded; sometimes a probate court is involved. The choices, and steps necessary to accomplish each, are discussed in Nissley, *How To Probate an Estate* (Nolo Press). Once the deceased owner's name is removed, this book can be used to transfer the property.

4. Complicated Transfers

As mentioned earlier, some types of transfers and real property issues are not discussed in this book. For instance, it is possible to transfer real property to someone only for his lifetime (this is called a life estate) or with conditions on ownership (e.g., no liquor may be served on the premises). For this kind of arrangement, custom-drafted documents, which are beyond the scope of this book, are necessary.

Also, occasionally ownership of property is confused or disputed and must be cleared up (a court proceeding may even be necessary) before a transfer is made. For example, if someone has brought a lawsuit against you claiming that the deed by which you acquired title to the property was fraudulent, you can't transfer the property until the "cloud" of the lawsuit is removed. If you have a problem or situation that we don't cover, you may need to consult a real estate expert or an attorney.

5. Mobile Homes

Only mobile homes that have been installed on a foundation are considered real property and thus can be transferred by deed. Mobile homes and manufactured houses that are not installed on a foundation approved by the State Department of Housing and Community Development are transferred by a title document, like the title to a car. When the mobile home is put on an approved foundation (a building permit is required), a local agency issues a certificate of occupancy and records, with the county recorder, a document stating that a mobile home has been affixed to real estate. The Department of Housing cancels the registration, and the owner gives the certificate of title back to the Department. From then on, the mobile home is transferred by a deed to the land it is situated on.

C. HOW TO USE THE BOOK IN SOME COMMON SITUATIONS

Here are some examples of common property transfers, to illustrate some of the ways this book can be used.

1. Giving Property to Adult Children

Emma and Alex want their son Walter to inherit their property, and they think it wise for estate planning purposes to transfer title of their house to Walter and his wife Eve now. Reading the background information about property law in Chapter 2, they discover that they may have to file a gift tax return (but not pay any tax now) because of the value of the property.[5] But because the house is paid for, they don't need to worry about paying off a loan before they can transfer the property.

In Chapter 3, they learn that because their house is community property, they must both sign the deed transferring it. They then go to Chapter 4 to find out how Walter and Eve can take title to the house. They find that they have four choices—they can transfer the property to "the kids" as a 1) tenants in common, 2) joint tenants, 3) community property, or 4) just to their son as his separate property. After weighing the pros and cons, Emma, Alex, Walter and Eve decide to use the community property option. They then go to Chapter 6 for instructions on how to select and fill out a grant deed to actually make the transfer and Chapter 7 for details on how to record the deed.

_____

[5]Chapter 2 also discusses ways Emma and Alex can avoid gift taxes.

Recording requested by

WALTER SINCLAIR and EVE SINCLAIR
8714 Hayes Street
Pasadena, California 92408

and when recorded mail
this deed and tax statements to:

same as above

For recorder's use

GRANT DEED

☒ This transfer is exempt from the documentary transfer tax.
☐ The documentary transfer tax is $_____ and is computed on
    ☐ the full value of the interest or property conveyed.
    ☐ the full value less the value of liens or encumbrances remaining thereon at the time of sale.
The property is located in ☐ an unincorporated area ☒ the city of __Pasadena__.

For a valuable consideration, receipt of which is hereby acknowledged,

    ALEXANDER SINCLAIR and EMMA SINCLAIR, husband and wife,

hereby grant(s) to

    WALTER SINCLAIR and EVE SINCLAIR, as husband and wife,

the following real property in the City of __Pasadena__, County of __Los Angeles__, California:

    Portion of Lots 14 and 15, Block 3, of the Del Mar Tract, filed March 21, 1934, Map Book B, page 187, Los Angeles County records, described as follows:
    Beginning on the east line of Powell Street, distant thereon north 0° 45' west 59 feet from the southwest corner of Block 3; thence from the point of beginning north 0° 45' east along Powell Street 60 feet; thence southeast along the south line of Clay Street 113 feet to the point of beginning.

Date: __July 19, 19__   _Emma Sinclair_
                          Alexander Sinclair

State of California
County of __Los Angeles__ } ss.

On __July 19, 19___, _Emma Sinclair and Alexander Sinclair_, known to me or proved by satisfactory evidence to be the person(s) whose name(s) is/are subscribed above, personally appeared before me, a Notary Public for California, and acknowledged that __they__ executed this deed.

__Kimberly Johnson__   [SEAL]
Signature of Notary

2. Selling an Interest in Jointly Owned Property

Marta and David, neither of whom is married, own property together as tenants in common. Marta would rather have cash than the land, and David offers to buy her out. Reading Chapter 2 for background, they are happy to find that the transfer will not require the property to be reassessed for property tax purposes

They also learn, however, that the terms of the loan on the property contain a "due on sale" clause, which means that (at least in theory) the loan must be paid off when the sale is made. But because interest rates have gone down since that loan was made, Marta and David conclude that the bank will probably not call the loan. If it does, David is willing to refinance the house (something he's considering anyway to take advantage of lower rates); he'll get a new loan and pay the old one off.

Marta and David then go on to the sections in Chapters 3 and 4 and read the material on how unmarried persons can transfer property and take title to it. Finally they read Chapters 6 and 7, which provide instructions on preparing and recording a deed to make the transfer. A tear-out copy of the deed form they need is in the Appendix.

PASSING TITLE
FROM HARE TO HEIR

3. Putting Property in Trust for a Child

Henry is getting on in years and wants to pass some property to his grand-daughter, Ruth, when he dies. For the time being, however, he wants to keep control of the property. He has investigated using a revocable living (inter vivos) trust and decides that putting the property in this kind of trust for Ruth is the best way to avoid probate's delay and expense. After drawing up a trust document setting out the terms of the trust (not covered in this book), Henry is ready to actually transfer the property to the trust.

Recording requested by

Henry R. Parker
781 Hayes Ave.
Monterey, CA 93784

and when recorded mail
this deed and tax statements to:

same as above

For recorder's use

GRANT DEED

☒ This transfer is exempt from the documentary transfer tax.
☐ The documentary transfer tax is $_____ and is computed on
  ☐ the full value of the interest or property conveyed.
  ☐ the full value less the value of liens or encumbrances remaining thereon at the time of sale.
The property is located in ☒ an unincorporated area. ☐ the city of _____.

For a valuable consideration, receipt of which is hereby acknowledged,

    HENRY R. PARKER and HELEN C. PARKER, husband and wife,

hereby grant(s) to

    HENRY R. PARKER, trustee for RUTH ELLEN MATTHEWS,

the following real property in the City of xxx_____, County of _Monterey_____,
California:

    Lots 1 and 2 of the Vernon Park Tract, filed July 3, 1947,
    in Book 23 of Maps, at page 132, in the Office of the
    County Recorder of Monterey County, California.

Date: __November 2, 19__   _Henry R Parker_
                            Helen C. Parker
                            _____
                            _____

State of California
County of _Monterey_____) ss.

On _November 2, 19__, _Henry R. Parker and Helen C. Parker_____, known to me or
proved by satisfactory evidence to be the person(s) whose name(s) is/are subscribed above, personally
appeared before me, a Notary Public for California, and
acknowledged that __they__ executed this deed.

__Rose M. Kellogg_____   [SEAL]
Signature of Notary

GRANT DEED

☐ This transfer is exempt from the documentary transfer tax.
☒ The documentary transfer tax is $ _200.00_ and is computed on
    ☐ the full value of the interest or property conveyed.
    ☒ the full value less the value of liens or encumbrances remaining thereon at the time of sale.
The property is located in ☐ an unincorporated area. ☒ the city of _San Francisco_ .

For a valuable consideration, receipt of which is hereby acknowledged,

Marta A. Richardson and David North, tenants in common,

hereby grant(s) to

David North, an unmarried man,

the following real property in the City of _San Francisco_ , County of _San Francisco_ , California:

Beginning at a point on the easterly line of Casey Way, distant thereon 200 feet south from the south line of 4th Avenue; thence south and along said line of Casey Way 25 feet; thence at a right angle east 130 feet; thence at a right angle north 25 feet; thence at a right angle west 130 feet to the point of beginning.

Being a part of Outside Land Block No. 440.

Date: _June 14, 19___   _David North_

                          Marta A. Richardson

State of California
County of _San Francisco_) ss.

On _June 14, 19___ , _David North and Marta A. Richardson_ , known to me or proved by satisfactory evidence to be the person(s) whose name(s) is/are subscribed above, personally appeared before me, a Notary Public for California, and acknowledged that _they_ executed this deed.

Kimberly Johnson   [SEAL]
Signature of Notary

Recording requested by
David North
46 Casey Way
San Francisco, CA 94122

and when recorded mail
this deed and tax statements to:

same as above

For recorder's use

First, he reads Chapter 2 for important background information. Among other things, he finds that the transfer to the trust will not trigger a reassessment for local property tax purposes or a due on sale loan clause. Because Henry is married, he checks Chapter 3 on transfers from married persons and then goes to the Chapter 4 section on transfers to trusts. That chapter explains the process and sends him to Chapters 6 and 7 for instructions on how to fill out and record the deed.

4. Executing a Deed of Trust on Property to Guarantee Payment of a Debt

Jeffrey wants to buy some land his parents own. His parents give him a good deal and offer to let him pay in installments. After reading Chapter 2, Jeffrey and his parents realize that their task is relatively simple; they don't need to worry about disclosure requirements or gift taxes, for example. Chapter 5 shows them how to prepare two of the three documents they will need: a promissory note (a written promise by Jeffrey to pay his parents back) and a deed of trust on the property signed by Jeffrey.

Chapter 6 covers preparation of the third document, a grant deed that will transfer the property to Jeffrey from his parents. Chapter 7 shows how to record each of these documents. After they have been recorded, if Jeffrey defaults on the note, the trustee (a person named in the trust deed) has the power to sell the land and pay his parents what Jeffrey still owes them.

Recording requested by

and when recorded mail this deed and tax statements to:

John T. Callaway

7643 Alameda Boulevard
Sacramento, CA 95608

For recorder's use

DEED OF TRUST

Jeffrey S. Callaway , Trustor, hereby grants Best Title Company , Trustee, with power of sale, the following real property in the City of Sacramento , County of Sacramento , California:

SEE EXHIBIT A, ATTACHED HERETO

:

together with its rents, issues and profits, subject to the Beneficiary's rights to collect and apply rents, issues and profits, given by paragraph 10 of the provisions incorporated herein by reference.

This deed is executed to secure payment of the debt evidenced by a promissory note signed by Trustor May 18 , 19__ in favor of John T. Callaway , Beneficiary, in the sum of $ 50,000 .

Trustor agrees that by execution and delivery of the deed of trust and the note it secures that provisions one through 14 of the fictitious deed of trust recorded October 18, 1961 in Santa Barbara and Sonoma Counties and in all other counties October 23, 1961, as set out below, are adopted and incorporated herein and that Trustor will observe those provisions.

The fictitious deed of trust incorporated herein is recorded with the county recorder of each California county as follows:

COUNTY	BOOK	PAGE	COUNTY	BOOK	PAGE	COUNTY	BOOK	PAGE	COUNTY	BOOK	PAGE
Alameda	435	684	Kings	792	833	Placer	895	301	Shasta	684	528
Alpine	1	250	Lake	362	39	Plumas	151	5	Sierra	29	335
Amador	104	348	Lassen	171	471	Riverside	3005	523	Siskiyou	468	181
Butte	1145	1	Los Angeles	T2055	899	Sacramento	4331	62	Solano	1105	182
Calaveras	145	152	Madera	810	170	San Benito	271	383	Sonoma	1851	689
Colusa	296	617	Marin	1508	339	San Bernardino	5567	61	Stanislaus	1715	1456
Contra Costa	3978	47	Mariposa	77	292	San Francisco	A332	905	Sutter	572	297
Del Norte	78	414	Mendocino	579	530	San Joaquin	2470	311	Tehama	491	289
El Dorado	568	456	Merced	1547	538	San Luis Obispo	1151	12	Trinity	93	366
Fresno	4626	572	Modoc	184	851	San Mateo	4078	420	Tulare	2294	275
Glenn	422	184	Mono	52	429	Santa Barbara	1878	860	Tuolumne	135	47
Humboldt	657	527	Monterey	2194	538	Santa Clara	5336	342	Ventura	2062	386
Imperial	1091	501	Napa	639	86	Santa Cruz	1431	494	Yolo	653	245
Inyo	147	598	Nevada	305	320	San Diego	Series 2	Page	Yuba	334	486
Kern	3427	60	Orange	5889	611		Book 1961	183887			

A copy of any Notice of Default and any Notice of Sale under this deed of trust shall be mailed to Trustor at:

873 Maple Street, Sacramento, CA 95809

Date: May 19, 19__

Signature of Trustor

Signature of Trustor

State of California
County of SACRAMENTO] ss.

On MAY 19 19__ JEFFREY S. CALLAWAY , known to me or proved by satisfactory evidence to be the person(s) whose name(s) is are subscribed above, personally appeared before me, a Notary Public for California, and acknowledged that he executed this deed.

Signature of Notary

[SEAL]

C H A P T E R   2

An Overview of Real Property Transfers

This chapter provides an overview of the real property transfer process and discusses the important legal and practical questions you may need to understand before you start the paperwork to actually make your transfer.

Property transfers can have important legal and tax consequences that you may have overlooked. It pays to patiently go over the key issues, including property ownership, lender policies, title rules, tax implications of transfers, and California's real estate disclosure laws. You may even learn something that prompts you to change the way you make the transfer.

For example, here are some of the questions you should keep in mind when you transfer California real property:

• Will the transfer make loans on the property come due all at once?

• Will the property transfer you have in mind trigger a local property tax reassessment, causing an increase in the property tax ?

• Will the transfer necessitate filing a gift tax return with the IRS?

• Are the current owners legally obligated to make written disclosures to the new owner about defects in the property?

• If you transfer property and then declare bankruptcy soon after, could creditors have the transfer invalidated?

The good news is that few of these issues are likely to apply to your situation. Sections A and B of this chapter provide an overview of the real property transfer process and define some basic legal terms; the details are in Section C, The Law of Real Estate Transfers. Reading the first paragraph or two of each subsection of Section C should let you determine whether or not the material is relevant.

A. AN OVERVIEW OF THE TRANSFER PROCESS

Reduced to its bare essentials, the process of transferring a piece of California real estate involves these steps:

- establishing that you own the property and have the right to transfer it;
- evaluating the legal consequences of the transfer (taxes, loan payments, etc.),
- choosing the correct kind of deed,
- filling out the deed, signing it, and having the signatures notarized, and
- filing a copy of the deed with the county recorder (recording the deed), and paying whatever transfer taxes apply.

In addition, you may have to fill out disclosure statements, give property tax information to the county assessor, or fill out a gift tax return.

Viewed as a whole, the transfer process is not complicated, although there is a fair degree of detail that merits serious attention. The part of the transfer process that does require some thought and decisionmaking (issues of title, taxes, loans, and disclosures) comes before you get to the actual transfer.

B. UNDERSTANDING BASIC TERMINOLOGY

Before we go on, let's stop a minute and define a few important real estate terms. A much more complete glossary is in the back of the book.

1. Real Property

Real property (real estate) is land and things permanently attached to land—everything from houses and trees down to built-in appliances. Thus a mobile home that is installed on a foundation is usually considered real property. Anything that's not real property is "personal property." Personal property that has been permanently attached to a structure on the property (e.g., chandeliers or built-in bookshelves) is considered real property and automatically passes to the new owner under a deed, unless the parties to the transfer agree otherwise.

2. Ownership

"Ownership" of real property, as a legal concept, is more complicated than it may appear. Most people think of ownership as an absolute thing—you either own property or you don't. The law, however, sees property ownership as a package of distinct "ownership interests." This package can be split in certain ways, and pieces of property ownership given to different people. If ownership has been repeatedly divided, with various property interests parceled out to different people, deciding who owns a piece of real property may not be easy.

There are two common ways for ownership of property to be split. One is when ownership is shared at the same time. For instance, if you and your spouse, or you and your three sisters, own a house together, you each own part of the whole interest in the property.[1]

Other "interests" in property can also be shared at the same time. For example, a neighbor may own an easement—a legal right to use part of your land subject to certain conditions (for example, the right to run a water pipe or path over a certain part of the land). As an easement owner, the neighbor is in essence a "co-owner" (although he would never be referred to as such in normal conversation) and you must take his rights into consideration before you transfer the property. Put differently, you can only transfer what you own—and if a neighbor acquired part of your ownership rights in the form of a right-of-way across the land, there's nothing you can do about it now. When you transfer the land, the easement goes with it, and the new owner takes the property subject to the easement.

---

[1]Depending on how title to the property is held (i.e., how the ownership is structured —as a joint tenancy, tenancy in common, community property, etc.) the co-owners have different legal rights and responsibilities. See Chapter 4.

Someone with a lease on the property also has some of the rights of the owner—the right to possess the property during the term of the lease, of course, is the important one. He can transfer those rights (if the lease permits it). Similarly, the owner can transfer her ownership rights, but can't end or interfere with the rights of the person with the lease. In other words, the property is transferred subject to the lease.

Ownership can also be shared over time. For instance, a deed may specify that one person owns property only for a certain period of time (most frequently, his lifetime). If someone has such a "life estate," somebody else, by necessity, has an ownership interest in the property that will take effect after the first person dies.[2] This second person's ownership rights do *not* include the right to use the property while the first owner is alive. But the second owner may, for instance, require the first owner to maintain the property's value by keeping it in good shape and making property tax and mortgage payments.[3]

---

[2]These concepts, and the terminology that accompanies them, are leftovers from the English feudal system of land ownership, when real property was almost the only measure of wealth and power. It was common for ownership interests to be divided intricately among many heirs or other persons. Any interest in property, even though less than complete ownership, was still important.

You may still occasionally run across some of the old terms used to describe these different types of ownership. For instance, absolute ownership of all interests in a particular piece of real estate is referred to as a "fee simple" interest. An ownership interest that lasts only for the span of one's life is called a "life estate." And the ownership interest that takes effect after the life estate ends is called a "remainder" or "reversionary" interest.

[3]The legal relationship between the first tenant (called the life tenant) and the second tenant (called the "remainderman") is so complex that the preferable way to give someone the use of property for his lifetime is to establish a trust. This book doesn't show you how to create a life estate; for that, you will need the help of an expert.

WHEN CALIFORNIA WAS A BARGAIN

How does $1.25 (or nothing) an acre for California land sound? Unfortunately, you're almost a century and a half too late.

When the United States acquired California at the end of the Mexican-American War in 1848, it promised to respect the rights of landowners who had obtained title from the Mexican government. Everything else went to the United States government. A few years later, after California was admitted to the Union in 1850, federal law allowed settlers to squat on public land and then buy it for $1.25 an acre. The 1862 Homestead Act went even further, giving up to 160 acres to a settler who lived on it and cultivated it for five years.

---

3. Title

The owner of a piece of property is said to have "title" to it. Title is proof of ownership. In that sense, title is just a shorthand way of referring to ownership. However, the two terms are not synonymous. It is possible to change the title —the way in which property is owned—without changing who owns it. A simple change in title, not ownership, is common among family members. For instance, if before you married, you and your current spouse took title to property as tenants in common, you might now want to change it so that title is held as community property. You would continue to own the property together, but the change in the way you hold title would produce a different set of consequences when you or your spouse died. We discuss these kinds of transfers in more detail in Chapter 4. For now, just remember that you must determine not only who owns the property before and after the transfer, but also how all of these people hold title to the property.

4. Title Search

To find out who owns property and how they hold the title to it, the first step is to look at the deed, which shows the current owners. Deeds, however, do not reveal certain kinds of problems with title to property. To confirm ownership requires a title search—a search of all public records of the property. Usually done by a title insurance company, the search includes examining copies of all the deeds that have ever transferred it, easements granted over it, liens placed against it, and tax and court records.

Checking the public records is usually reliable because all ownership interests in land are supposed to be recorded with the county to be fully effective (the recording system is discussed in some detail in Chapter 7). All deeds passing the property from owner to owner should be on record.

Evidence of other interests in the land will most likely be in the form of a document granting an easement, giving the property as security for a loan, or announcing that someone has placed a lien on the property to insure payment of a debt or taxes.[4]

Title searches are routine whenever property is transferred and a bank or savings and loan is involved. Before making a loan that is secured by the property, a lender wants to make sure that the buyer is getting good title to it. Title searches are not necessary in some intra-family transfers or when owners just want to change the way they hold title (see Section D below).

5. Title Insurance

Title companies guarantee the results of their searches by issuing title insurance policies, usually in the amount of the value of the property. Title insurance protects an owner (or whoever loaned money to finance the purchase of the property) against losses that result from a defect in the title that exists when the policy is issued and is discovered later. For example, a typical title insurance policy would cover an owner's losses if any of the transfer documents are fraudulent or forged, or there is a lien or easement on the property that the title company didn't find when it searched the records. If an owner puts in a claim under the policy, the insurance company can, like any other insurance company, defend the owner in a lawsuit or negotiate a settlement.

In many private, intra-family transfers, where no institutional lender is financing the purchase and all the parties are confident that the title is clear,

---

[4]Unrecorded transfers, of course, don't show up in a title search. Also, some easements and community property interests arise under law and are valid even though they are not recorded. We cover this in more detail in Section D below.

they decide not to buy title insurance. In many situations, however, title insurance is a wise investment. Section D, below, discusses how to decide about title insurance and how to get it if you decide you want it.

6. Deeds

Deeds are the documents that transfer ownership of real property. In California, the most common kinds are grant, quitclaim, and trust deeds. Their functions are quite different. Here is a very brief overview of each:

Grant deed: The most commonly used type of deed. It contains guarantees that title being passed hasn't already been transferred to someone else or been encumbered (see Section 7 below), except as specified in the deed. The grantor is the person transferring the property; the grantee is the person receiving it.

Quitclaim deed: A deed that is used to give up one's claims to land. Unlike a grant deed, the quitclaim deed makes no promises about the title being transferred. The maker of a quitclaim deed simply transfers whatever interest in the land he may have at the time. Quitclaims are often used when someone has a theoretical claim to real property; the potential claimant gives up the claim and the property's owner doesn't have to worry about the claim being made later. They can also be used instead of a grant deed; they are just as effective to transfer ownership of property.

Trust deed (deed of trust): A trust deed is more like a mortgage than it is a grant or quitclaim deed. It isn't used to transfer ownership of property; it comes into play when someone uses real property as security for a loan—which is almost anytime someone buys real estate. It is used in conjunction with a promissory note (a written promise to pay back a loan). The buyer signs the note and a trust deed, which permits its holder (the trustee) to sell the property and pay off the loan if the buyer defaults.

7. Encumbrance

An encumbrance is any legal claim on property that affects an owner's ability to transfer title to the property. Common encumbrances are deeds of trust, mortgages, and past due property tax liens (claims filed against the property when property taxes are delinquent). If your property is encumbered—say, for example, there is a trust deed on the property because you borrowed money to buy it—before you can transfer title you will either have to remove the encumbrance (by paying off the loan secured by the trust deed) or get the buyer to agree to take the property subject to the encumbrance.[5]

Enough terminology. Don't despair if it seems like a short course in Greek; we'll redefine the important terms when you run across them again.

C. THE LAW OF PROPERTY TRANSFERS

Before you commit yourself to a transaction, you should know about the state and federal law (and, if the property is security for a loan, the regulations of private lenders) that may affect your property transfer. For our purposes— noncommercial transfers of real property and changes in the way title to real property is held—these laws and regulations fall into six main areas:

1. Existing deeds of trust or other encumbrances on the property, which may have to be paid off or transferred as part of the transaction.

2. Local property tax reassessment rules.

3. Federal gift tax regulations.

4. California and local real estate transfer disclosure requirements.

5. Local transfer taxes.

6. Laws penalizing transfers made to defraud creditors.

On April 1, 1987, the IRS issued regulations requiring a new form, No. 1099-R, to be filed when a home is sold. The form was not yet available when this book went to press.

---

[5]In the case of a trust deed, you would most likely also have to get the approval of the lender for the new owner to take over the loan.

1. Encumbrances

First, the good news for readers whose transfer is uncomplicated by encumbrances. You can skip this discussion and go to subsection 2 if:

• the property being transferred has no existing deeds of trust, mortgages, past due property taxes or homeowners' association assessments, liens or other encumbrances on its title (e.g., the property is owned outright, free of ownership or lien claims by others and property tax payments are up-to-date[6]); **or**

• the owner(s) want only to change the form in which title is held (e.g., from tenancy in common to joint tenancy, or from a single owner to a revocable trust with the owner as trustee), and the identity of the owners doesn't change.

Note: If money is changing hands for the property, or a new owner is involved, or if you really don't know for sure whether or not there are encumbrances, it is wise to investigate just how clear the transferor's title to the property really is. That's when you need a title search (see Section D below).

a. Deeds and Encumbrances

When you use a grant deed (the kind of deed used most often in California) to transfer property, you automatically promise that you have disclosed to the new owner all encumbrances you have incurred.[7] If you do not disclose the existence of such an encumbrance, you can be liable for the new owner's damages. For example, if the grantor neglects to tell the buyer that there is a huge tax lien on the property, the buyer can sue him for what it costs to pay off the lien.

Under the law, the encumbrances about which a grantor must tell the grantee, when transferring property with a grant deed, include taxes, assessments, and liens on the property.[8] For example, if a carpenter who worked on a house has recorded a mechanic's lien on the property to insure that he is paid, the grantor must disclose it. Otherwise a recipient would take title to the property subject to the lien, which could mean that if the grantor doesn't pay the carpenter, the carpenter could have the house sold to pay off the debt.[9]

---

[6]If, like most homeowners, you borrowed money to buy your house and executed a deed of trust securing the loan, title to the property is encumbered. Past due property taxes are another fairly common encumbrance.

[7]Civil Code § 1113.

[8]Civil Code § 1114.

[9]The grantor does not promise that he has good title to the property. The grantor is not responsible for other claims on the property that aren't based on acts of the grantor and are out of his control. The most common examples of such claims (none of them is very common) are claims by someone whose claim arose under a former owner, and eminent domain (condemnation) proceedings by government entities. Thus if you receive a grant deed to property and then find out there are condemnation proceedings

Because buyers (and lenders) do not usually want to rely on the seller's disclosure and implied promise, they routinely order title searches and purchase title insurance. If a problem with the title (including an encumbrance that they didn't know about when they bought) is discovered later, the insurance will pay, and they don't have to sue (and try to collect from) the grantor.

b. Taking Care of Encumbrances

Most encumbrances can simply be paid off, leaving title to the property clear and free to be transferred. The most obvious example is the deed of trust. When you want to transfer property that is subject to a trust deed, you must do one of three things: pay it off, get the buyer to assume the loan, or get the buyer to take the property "subject to" the deed of trust. Assumption of a loan, which means that the new owner takes responsibility for paying it off, is handled through the bank. Your loan agreement with the financial institution, however, may have a "due on sale" clause, which limits who can assume a loan secured by the property (see box below). If the new owner takes the property "subject to" the loan, he acknowledges the loan (by including a statement in the deed) but doesn't formally assume it. If the note were foreclosed on, however, he would lose the property.

Note: Even if the property is not encumbered, a lien can appear out of thin air if the new owner has an outstanding court judgment against him. When the transfer is made, the judgment lien attaches to the property. Transferring the property back won't get rid of the lien.

underway, you're out of luck as far as suing under the promise that the statute says is implied in the grant deed.

DUE ON SALE CLAUSES

Many loan agreements contain a "due on sale" or "due on transfer" clause that makes the whole loan amount due immediately if the property is sold. And even if the existing loan can be assumed by the new owners, the terms of the loan probably require the new owners to get approval from the lender.

If a lender's approval is necessary, whether or not you will get it will probably have a lot to do with market interest rates. It makes sense that if interest rates have come down since the trust deed was signed, the lender will be happy to have a buyer (who has good credit) take over the loan at the relatively high interest rate. On the other hand, if rates have gone up, it will probably insist on a new loan at a higher rate of interest. If the original loan is a variable-rate loan, the lender has little incentive to be finicky unless market rates have exceeded even the maximum allowed by terms of the variable-rate loan. For this reason, variable-rate loans are often assumable.

"In the event the herein described property or any part thereof, or any interest therein is sold, agreed to be sold, conveyed or alienated by the Trustor, or by the operation of law or otherwise, all obligations secured by this instrument, irrespective of the maturity dates expressed therein, at the option of the older hereof and without demand or notice shall immediately become due and payable."

Many people who own real property subject to a trust deed simply go ahead and transfer it, figuring the lender (who, after all, may be a large corporation at the other end of the country that bought the trust deed from a local bank), won't find out. They are often right.

Lenders do, however, have several ways to discover that the property was transferred, even if you don't tell them. A change in the name of the person making loan payments or named as beneficiary on the insurance policy often alerts a bank. Sometimes they simply call and ask for the original borrower; if the new owner says she doesn't live there, the game is up. The lender can also check (or pay someone to check) county records to see if title to the property has changed hands.

How diligent the bank is largely depends, again, on interest rates. Unless rates have gone up significantly (2% is a good rule of thumb) since a fixed-rate loan was made, it isn't worth it to check title records all over the country to see if property has been sold. When interest rates shoot up quickly, however, and an investor holds a lot of fixed-rate loans, you can bet it is looking for transfers that will allow it to call those loans. The financial institution's policy also plays a part; some regularly use a title company to keep an eye on transfers.

Some people, to avoid notifying a bank of a transfer, don't record the deed in the county recorder's office. This is a bad idea, for all the reasons explained in Chapter 7. Experienced real estate lawyers can sometimes manage ways to get around due-on-sale clauses and still effectively transfer property. If a due-on-sale clause is a serious problem for you, talk to a lawyer.

Other simple money encumbrances include:

• past due property taxes (due and payable twice each year, in November and February).

• mechanic's or materialman's liens,[10] filed by persons who work on your house.

• unpaid special assessment district bond liens (e.g., imposed by special hospital or drainage districts).

• judgment liens (liens placed against your property to guarantee payment of a judgment against you in a lawsuit).[11]

A more complicated encumbrance is a lawsuit that may affect title to your property. It shows up in the public records when a notice of the suit (a "lis pendens") is recorded in the county recorder's office. You can't get rid of this kind of encumbrance by simply paying it off. You must, however, deal with it somehow, either by passing it on to the new owner, negotiating a settlement with the party who has the claim against your property, or—if you absolutely can't avoid it—going to court to slug it out. A common method of settlement is to pay the other party something in exchange for a quitclaim deed in which she gives up any interest that she might own in the property.

Example: Andy and his brother Bill inherited some land from their uncle, but the uncle's will is being disputed in court by their cousin, Marsha. Depending on the outcome of the suit, Marsha may be determined to have some interest in the land. Andy wants to sell his half-interest to Bill, but title to the property is encumbered by a notice of the lawsuit (a "lis pendens"), which has been recorded with the county recorder. For payment of a few thousand dollars, Marsha agrees to drop the lawsuit and sign a quitclaim deed giving up all rights to the property. With the encumbrance removed, Bill can take clear title to the property.

---

[10]A lien is a notice, recorded with the county recorder, that alerts everyone to the fact that there is a claim against the property.

[11]If the owner of the property has recorded a declaration of homestead for the property, the house legally can be sold with the lien as long as the proceeds of the sale (up to the level protected by the homestead law) are invested in another residence within six months. Homesteads are discussed in Chapter 7, Section D.

2. Property Tax Reassessment

Many real estate transfers trigger a reassessment of the property for local property tax purposes. And, although property taxes are limited by the state constitution (that's what Proposition 13 did), reassessment usually means a higher assessed value and a higher property tax bill. If it's not transferred, property is usually reassessed once a year according to a standard formula that allows an increase of up to two percent in the assessed value of the property. If it is sold, however, the assessor uses the sale price as the basis for reassessment.

State law exempts some kinds of transfers from the reassessment requirement. If, under state law, a transfer is not considered a "change of ownership," the property is not subject to reassessment. Many intra-family transfers of the type discussed in this book do not trigger reassessment, including:[12]

• A transfer between spouses, or one that takes effect at the death of one spouse or at dissolution of the marriage.

Example: When Allen marries Maureen, he wants to add her name to the title of his house, so he signs a deed from himself to both of them. The house will not be reassessed.

• Correction of a deed.

Example: When Denise makes out a deed to Paula, she mistakenly types "Paul" instead. To correct this mistake, which could cause confusion later on, she makes a new deed with the correct name.

• A transfer to a revocable living trust, or by the trustee back to the person who set up the trust.

Example: Don wants to put some property in a living trust for his children so they will inherit it outside probate when he dies. He signs a grant deed to formally transfer the property to the trust.

• Any transfer between co-owners that changes only the method of holding title, without changing the proportional interests of the co-owners.

---

[12]Rev. & Tax. Code §§ 62, 63. Some other transfers are included; we list only the situations that are covered in this book.

Example: Ray and his cousin Lee inherited property in joint tenancy, which carries with it an automatic right of survivorship. They want to change the way title is held to a tenancy in common so that each can leave his share to his spouse.[13] To do this, they execute a deed from themselves as joint tenants to themselves as tenants in common. No reassessment will be made.

• Creation of a joint tenancy *if* one of the original owners is one of the new joint tenants.

Example: Martha wants to put title to her house in joint tenancy with her daughter. She executes a deed from herself to her daughter and herself as joint tenants.

• Execution of a deed of trust.

Example: Frank wants to borrow money from his parents, using his house as security for the loan. Frank signs a deed of trust, giving a trustee the power to sell the house and pay off the loan to his parents if he defaults.

• Transfer between former spouses in connection with a property settlement agreement or decree of dissolution of marriage.

Example: Luke and Lisa are divorced. The property settlement agreement states that Lisa will transfer her interest in the couple's house to Luke.

• Transfer of the transferor's principal residence (and up to $1 million of other real property), in a transfer between parents and their children.

Example: Sarah and Ben want to transfer title to some land they own to their children. As long as their equity in the land is less than $1 million, they can transfer it without triggering a reassessment.

If your property will be reassessed, the county assessor will send you (after you record your deed) a Change in Ownership Statement. Instructions for filling it out are in Chapter 7.

---

[13]To leave the property to their spouses, each would have to make a will or use another estate planning device (such as a living trust).

3. Gifts of Real Property: Federal Gift Tax

If a gift of real property is large enough, the giver may have to file a federal gift tax return. You don't have to worry about gift tax, and can proceed directly to subsection 4 below, if the property being transferred:

• is being sold for its approximate fair market value,[14] or

• is being given away, but the value of the equity[15] being given is less than $10,000 per recipient ($20,000 if a married couple is giving it) or

• is being given by one spouse to the other.

WHAT IF YOU'RE NOT SURE YOUR TRANSFER IS EXEMPT?

You may want to file a gift tax return even if you think your transaction is exempt from tax. Filing a return can give you some peace of mind if you worry that the IRS might someday challenge your claim to exemption.

For example, say you think the property you're giving your son has a fair market value of $10,000 and is thus exempt from gift tax. How do you know that the IRS, years later, won't decide that the fair market value was $17,000 and that you should have filed a gift tax return? After all, fair market value is sometimes an inexact concept.

If you file a gift tax return announcing that the transaction is exempt, the IRS has three years to challenge it. If you don't file a return, it could still contest the tax status of the transfer years later, when you die and your final gift/estate tax is calculated.

Because this is a book on transfers, not taxes, we don't try to cover the subject of gift taxes in detail. What we can do is alert you to potential problems and outline strategies you may want to pursue. With that warning, here are the basics of federal gift tax law.

---

[14]This is the amount your house could fetch if sold on the open market. This figure can be derived from what comparable houses are sold for or, if necessary, from an appraiser. You can also go by the value placed on the house by the local property tax assessor, if the assessment is relatively recent and the assessment is intended to be full market value.

[15]To figure equity, subtract the amount owed on the property (deeds of trust and other encumbrances) from the total value of the property.

a. Overview of the Federal Unified Gift and Estate Tax

Federal tax laws have long seen people with accumulated wealth as fair game for taxation. The federal gift/estate tax[16] strikes when a property owner gets rid of his property either by giving it away or leaving it when he dies—which manages to get just about everybody.

True to its name, the tax is levied on gifts and estates alike. The tax rate is the same whether the property is given before or after death. By taxing property that's given before death, the gift tax thwarts people who try to avoid the estate tax by giving their property away before they die.

Some gifts are always exempt from gift taxation. Gifts of any amount to a spouse, to a tax-exempt organization, or for medical expenses or school tuition can be made tax-free. See section d below.

b. What Is a Gift?

Sometimes you may not be positive whether or not the transfer you are making is in fact a gift. A gift, in the eyes of the law, is any voluntary transfer of property made without receiving anything, (or receiving less than its value), in exchange.[17] For example, if you transfer property that you know is worth $50,000 to your son and take $10,000 in exchange, you have made a gift of $40,000.

Generally, a transfer is not a gift unless you intend it to be. But the IRS doesn't know, when you transfer something for less than its market value, whether you intend to make a gift or you're just a poor businessperson. So it does the only thing it can do—it looks at the objective evidence and demands gift taxes only if a transaction doesn't appear reasonable from an economic point of view. Don't expect the IRS to accept your simple statement that, despite every indication to the contrary, your transfer of a house to your son for $1 is just a bargain, not a gift. You will be held to have intended a gift when you know at the time that you are taking less than the fair market value for the property.

---

[16]There is no state gift or estate tax in California.

[17]The legal term for what is given in exchange is "consideration."

The legal elements of a gift are:

1. The giver (donor) must be competent;

2. The giver must intend to make a gift;

3. The gift must be delivered;

4. The gift must be accepted by the recipient (donee);

5. The giver must give up all control over the gift; and

6. The recipient must not give anything in exchange (consideration) for the gift (or the consideration is far less than the value of the gift).

You must satisfy requirements 1, 3, 4, and 5 any time you transfer real property via a deed (see Chapter 6), so all you need worry about when you want to make a gift are the other two requirements (2 and 6), discussed above.

c. How the Gift Tax Works

Congress has decided that you are entitled to give away (by giving it away while you're living or leaving it in your estate when you die) at least $600,000 tax-free.[18] This means that as a practical matter, most people don't ever have to shell out money for gift or estate taxes because they don't give away and leave a total of more than $600,000 of property.

Because your liability for estate and gift taxation cannot be figured until you have either died or given away $600,000 in non-exempt gifts, [19] you don't pay taxes on gifts when you make them unless the $600,000 figure has been exceeded. On the other hand, every time you make a non-exempt gift, it reduces the amount of the $600,000 exemption you have left.

If you make non-exempt gifts, you don't have the option of going ahead and paying the tax now, saving your $600,000 exempt amount for property you leave when you die. Thus although you may have to file a gift tax return if you make a gift of real property by transferring it to someone else or adding someone's name to the title, it is extremely unlikely that you will have to pay any tax now.

Example: During his lifetime, Frank makes non-exempt gifts that total $28,000. When he dies, $572,000 of his estate will go to his heirs and beneficiaries without being subject to the estate tax.

---

[18]Actually, this amount can be much higher, because, as we point out later, any gift to a single recipient in any one year that is $10,000 or less, and gifts for certain purposes such as medical care and education, don't count as gifts at all for tax purposes.

[19]Exemptions are explained below.

d. What Gifts Are Taxable

Any gift worth more than $10,000 given to one person in one year is subject to the federal gift tax. (Remember, the giver, not the recipient, is taxed.) Each member of a married couple gets the $10,000 exclusion, so together they can give up to $20,000 per recipient without reducing either's $600,000 exemption amount.

Example 1: Joe gives real estate in which he has equity of $10,000 to each of his three children. He need not file a gift tax return.

Example 2: Robin gives her son Ralph $6,000 in cash and $10,000 in real estate in one calendar year. Because the total is over the $10,000 limit, she must file a gift tax return for the excess. She will not have to pay tax but will use part of her $600,000 credit, leaving a $594,000 credit when she dies (assuming she makes no more non-exempt gifts). Had Robin waited until January 1 of the next year to give the real estate, both gifts would have been entirely exempt.

Example 3: In 1987, Anne and her husband Peter give real estate worth $120,000 and subject to a deed of trust for $80,000 to their daughter Sophie and her husband Jeff. The total value of the gift is thus $40,000. Anne and Peter do not need to file a gift tax return. Anne and Peter each can give $10,000 per recipient, and there are two recipients, so $40,000 is exempt.

As mentioned above, some types of gifts are always exempt: gifts made to one's spouse or to tax-exempt organizations are always tax-free, no matter what the amount. So are gifts made for medical bills or school tuition.

Example: Francine owns a large undeveloped tract of land that is home to a diverse group of animals and plants, some of them rare. To preserve its wild state, she gives the land to the Nature Conservancy, a tax-exempt organization that acquires land to help preserve native animal and plant life. Her equity in the property is $620,000. The gift is exempt from gift taxes, so it doesn't affect her $600,000 credit.

e. Figuring the Tax Rate

The gift tax rate (which, again, is the same as the federal estate tax rate) increases with the amount of the gift. The more you give, the higher the percentage of the gift you must ultimately pay in gift tax.

Gift tax returns must be filed when the taxpayer files her regular annual income tax return. You must file a gift tax return if you give away more than

$10,000 to one person (not including a tax-exempt organization), even if you do not, because of the tax credit, have to pay any tax. The returns can be tricky, and you may well want to consult a tax preparer or tax attorney before you file one.

f. Avoiding or Lowering Gift Taxes on Real Estate Transfers

Not surprisingly, people have figured out some clever ways to reduce or avoid their gift and estate tax liability. For example, a husband and wife may want to give their house to their son before they die in order to avoid the delay and expense of having the house pass through probate. They must pay gift tax (in the form of a reduction of their $600,000 credit) on the value of the gift (that is, their equity in the house) over the couple's $20,000 annual exemption. However, if they loan their son the price of the house, transfer the house subject to a mortgage, and then forgive the mortgage payments as they come due (i.e., make a gift of them), they avoid paying gift taxes as long as the mortgage payments (the gifts) are less than $20,000 per year.[20]

Another way to do it, depending on the amount of equity in the property, is for the owners to put property in joint tenancy with the intended recipient (this is a gift of half the equity in the property) and then, the next calendar year, transfer the remaining half-interest.

We don't get into all the complexities of this subject here. If large amounts of money are involved, see a good tax accountant.

4. Disclosure Requirements

California law may require you to make several kinds of written disclosures about the condition of the property to the new owners before the transfer goes through. You need to make one or more of these disclosures if the transfer is a sale of residential property with one to four units, or the property is in a state-designated "special studies" (earthquake fault) zone, *unless*

• the transfer is a gift, or

• the transfer is to a co-owner, spouse, former spouse, or direct descendant or ancestor,[21]

• the transfer is from a trustee, guardian, or conservator.

---

[20]This example comes from Denis Clifford's *Plan Your Estate* (Nolo Press), which we recommend that you read if you want to delve into the subject of gift-giving as an estate planning device.

[21]Under this rule, uncles and aunts, brothers and sisters, and cousins are not exempt, since they are not direct descendants.

Sometimes, cities and counties add their own disclosure requirements. Even if you're not required to make disclosures under state law, check subsection b below to see if local requirements apply.

a. Real Estate Transfer Disclosure Statement

If you're selling residential (not commercial) real property, you will probably have to disclose to the buyer certain information about the property's condition.[22] The disclosure covers all major structures and systems on the property. For example, you must tell the buyer of significant defects in the driveway, electrical system, plumbing, roof, and foundation. If the buyer doesn't like what he learns, the law gives him three days to back out of the sale.

If your transfer is a sale and does not fit within one of the exemptions listed above, you will have to fill out the disclosure form shown below. A tear-out copy is included in the Appendix.

The completed form must be personally delivered or mailed to the buyer before title is transferred. The buyer has three days after the form is delivered (five days after the date of mailing, if the form was mailed) to give the seller a written withdrawal of his offer to purchase the property.[23]

The seller is responsible for disclosing only information that is in his personal knowledge—that is, he doesn't have to hire professionals to answer the questions on the disclosure form. The seller must, however, fill out the form in good faith and honestly and must take "ordinary care" in obtaining the information. This means that the seller is responsible for including information about the property that he knows or, as a reasonable homeowner, should know.

---

[22]Civil Code § 1102.

[23]Civil Code § 1102.2.

REAL ESTATE TRANSFER DISCLOSURE STATEMENT

THIS DISCLOSURE STATEMENT CONCERNS THE REAL PROPERTY SITUATED IN THE CITY OF _____, COUNTY OF _____, STATE OF CALIFORNIA, DESCRIBED AS _____ _____. THIS STATEMENT IS A DISCLOSURE OF THE CONDITION OF THE ABOVE DESCRIBED PROPERTY IN COMPLIANCE WITH SECTION 1102 OF THE CIVIL CODE AS OF _____, 19____. IT IS NOT A WARRANTY OF ANY KIND BY THE SELLER(S) OR ANY AGENT(S) REPRESENTING ANY PRINCIPAL(S) IN THIS TRANSACTION, AND IS NOT A SUBSTITUTE FOR ANY INSPECTIONS OR WARRANTIES THE PRINCIPAL(S) MAY WISH TO OBTAIN.

I

COORDINATION WITH OTHER DISCLOSURE FORMS

This Real Estate Transfer Disclosure Statement is made pursuant to Section 1102 of the Civil Code. Other statutes require disclosures, depending upon the details of the particular real estate transaction (for example: special study zone and purchase-money liens on residential property).

Substituted Disclosures: The following disclosures have or will be made in connection with this real estate transfer, and are intended to satisfy the disclosure obligations on this form, where the subject matter is the same: _____

_____
_____
_____

(list all substituted disclosure forms to be used in connection with this transaction)

II

SELLERS INFORMATION

The Seller discloses the following information with the knowledge that even though this is not a warranty, prospective Buyers may rely on this information in deciding whether and on what terms to purchase the subject property. Seller hereby authorizes any agent(s) representing any principal(s) in this transaction to provide a copy of this statement to any person or entity in connection with any actual or anticipated sale of the property.

THE FOLLOWING ARE REPRESENTATIONS MADE BY THE SELLER(S) AND ARE NOT THE REPRESENTATIONS OF THE AGENT(S), IF ANY. THIS INFORMATION IS A DISCLOSURE AND IS NOT INTENDED TO BE PART OF ANY CONTRACT BETWEEN THE BUYER AND SELLER.

Seller __is __is not occupying the property.

A. The subject property has the items checked below (read across):

__Range   __Oven   __Microwave
__Dishwasher   __Trash Compactor   __Garbage Disposal
__Washer/Dryer Hookups __Window Screens   __Rain Gutters
__Burglar Alarms   __Smoke Detector(s)   __Fire Alarm
__T.V. Antenna   __Satellite Dish   __Intercom
__Central Heating   __Central Air Cndtng. __Evaporator Cooler(s)
__Wall/Window Air Cndtng. __Sprinklers   __Public Sewer System
__Septic Tank   __Sump Pump   __Water Softener
__Patio/Decking   __Built-in Barbeque   __Gazebo
__Sauna   __Pool   __Spa __Hot Tub
__Security Gate(s)   __Garage Door Opener(s) __Number Remote Controls

Garage: __Attached   __Not Attached   __Carport
Pool/Spa Heater: __Gas __Solar   __Electric
Water Heater: __Gas   __Private Utility or
Water Supply: __City   __Well
Gas Supply: __Utility __Bottled   Other _____

Exhaust Fan(s) in _____ 220 Volt Wiring in _____ Fireplace(s) in _____ Gas Starter _____
Roof(s): Type: _____ Age: _____ (approx.)
Other: _____
Are there, to the best of your (Seller's) knowledge, any of the above that are not in operating condition? __Yes __No. If yes, then describe. (Attach additional sheets if necessary.): _____
_____
_____

B. Are you (Seller) aware of any significant defects/malfunctions in any of the following? __Yes __No. If yes, check appropriate space(s) below.

__Interior Walls __Ceilings __Floors __Exterior Walls __Insulation __Roof(s) __Windows __Doors __Foundation __Slab(s) __Driveways __Sidewalks __Walls/Fences __Electrical Systems __Plumbing/Sewers/Septics __Other Structural Components (Describe: _____

If any of the above is checked, explain. (Attach additional sheets if necessary): _____
_____
_____
_____

C. Are you (Seller) aware of any of the following:

1. Features of the property shared in common with adjoining landowners, such as walls, fences, and driveways, whose use or responsibility for maintenance may have an effect on the subject property .... __Yes __No
2. Any encroachments, easements or similar matters that may affect your interest in the subject property .... __Yes __No

3. Room additions, structural modifications, or other alterations or repairs made without necessary permits .... __Yes __No
4. Room additions, structural modifications, or other alterations or repairs not in compliance with building codes .... __Yes __No
5. Landfill (compacted or otherwise) on the property or any portion thereof .... __Yes __No
6. Any settling from any cause, or slippage, sliding, or other soil problems ...... __Yes __No
7. Flooding, drainage or grading problems............................... __Yes __No
8. Major damage to the property or any of the structures from fire, earthquake, floods, or landslides .... __Yes __No
9. Any zoning violations, nonconforming uses, violations of "setback" requirements .... __Yes __No
10. Neighborhood noise problems or other nuisances .... __Yes __No
11. CC&R's or other deed restrictions or obligations .... __Yes __No
12. Homeowners' Association which has any authority over the subject property .... __Yes __No
13. Any "common area" (facilities such as pools, tennis courts, walkways, or other areas co-owned in undivided interest with others)................ __Yes __No
14. Any notices of abatement or citations against the property .... __Yes __No
15. Any lawsuits against the seller threatening to or affecting this real property .... __Yes __No

If the answer to any of these is yes, explain. (Attach additional sheets if necessary.): _____
_____
_____
_____

Seller certifies that the information herein is true and correct to the best of the Seller's knowledge as of the date signed by the Seller.

Seller _____
Date _____

Seller _____
Date _____

III
AGENTS INSPECTION DISCLOSURE
(Please Print)

IV
AGENTS INSPECTION DISCLOSURE
(To be completed only if the agent who has obtained the offer is other than the agent above.)
THE UNDERSIGNED, BASED ON A REASONABLY COMPETENT AND DILIGENT VISUAL INSPECTION OF THE ACCESSIBLE AREAS OF THE PROPERTY, STATES THE FOLLOWING:
(Please Print)

V
BUYER(S) AND SELLER(S) MAY WISH TO OBTAIN PROFESSIONAL ADVICE AND/OR INSPECTIONS OF THE PROPERTY AND TO PROVIDE FOR APPROPRIATE PROVISIONS IN A CONTRACT BETWEEN BUYER AND SELLER(S) WITH RESPECT TO ANY ADVICE/INSPECTIONS/DEFECTS.

(To be completed only if the seller is represented by an agent in this transaction.)

THE UNDERSIGNED, BASED ON THE ABOVE INQUIRY OF THE SELLER(S) AS TO THE CONDITION OF THE PROPERTY AND BASED ON A REASONABLY COMPETENT AND DILIGENT

VISUAL INSPECTION OF THE ACCESSIBLE AREAS OF THE PROPERTY IN CONJUNCTION WITH THAT INQUIRY, STATES THE FOLLOWING: _____
_____
_____

Agent (Broker
Representing Seller) _____ By _____ Date
_____
(Associate Licensee or Broker-Signature)

_____
_____
_____
_____

Agent (Broker
obtaining the Offer) _____ By _____ Date
_____
(Associate Licensee or Broker-Signature)

I/WE ACKNOWLEDGE RECEIPT OF A COPY OF THIS STATEMENT.
Seller _____ Date _____ Buyer
_____ Date _____
Seller _____ Date _____ Buyer
_____ Date _____

Agent (Broker
Representing Seller) _____ By _____ Date
_____
(Associate Licensee or Broker-Signature)

Agent (Broker
obtaining the Offer) _____ By _____ Date
_____
(Associate Licensee or Broker-Signature)

A REAL ESTATE BROKER IS QUALIFIED TO ADVISE ON REAL ESTATE. IF YOU DESIRE LEGAL ADVICE, CONSULT YOUR ATTORNEY.

If you don't know and can't find out (by making a reasonable effort) some of the information requested on the form, you may make a "reasonable approximation" as long as you make it clear (on the form) that the information is an approximation that is based on the best information available to you.

If an error or omission is carelessly or intentionally made in the statement, the sale is still valid, but the seller is liable for any actual damages the buyer suffers. For example, if you sell your house and forget to disclose the fact that the roof leaks (and you know or should know it does), the sale is still good, but if the buyer sues you, you'll have to pay for the damage that the leak causes and the cost of repairs.

You should take seriously your responsibility to disclose problems and err on the side of more, rather than less, disclosure. Many homeowners, although it is not required by the law, are choosing to protect themselves by hiring (or encouraging the buyer to hire) a general contractor to inspect the house and write a report on its condition. Home-inspection firms are popping up in response to the demand. An inspection and written report for an average-sized house costs from about $175 to $300. If you do get a report, make sure the new owner gets a copy and you get written acknowledgment that she did.

b. Special Studies Zone (Earthquake Fault) Disclosure

You must also tell prospective purchasers if your property is within a state-designated "special studies zone."[24] Special studies zones are areas along earthquake faults identified by state geologists. These designations are often puzzling; for example, San Francisco is not within a special study zone.

To find out if the property you want to transfer is within a special studies zone, check with your local city or county planning department. It should have state maps that show the areas.

The statute says owners must disclose the special studies zone information to "any prospective purchaser," which includes just about everybody. We suggest giving the following disclosure form to serious prospective purchasers. Just be sure to give it to a buyer before the actual transfer takes place.

[24]Public Resources Code § 2621.9.

SPECIAL STUDIES ZONE DISCLOSURE

The real property at _____,
_____ County, California, lies within a special studies
zone designated by the California Department of Geology.

This disclosure is made under Public Resources Code § 2621.9.

_____   _____, 19____
Transferor

I acknowledge that I have received a copy of this disclosure form.

_____   _____, 19____
Transferee

After you give the disclosure form to the buyer, have him sign the acknowledgment at the bottom of the form, and keep a copy (or have him sign two copies, one for you to keep). A tear-out form is included in the Appendix.

c. Local Real Property Transfer Requirements

Some cities impose their own requirements on real estate transfers. For example, sellers may be required to advise buyers of applicable zoning laws (Los Angeles has this requirement) or the property may need to pass local energy efficiency standards. To find out if the property you want to transfer is subject to any such local rules, ask your city planning department.

5. Documentary Transfer Tax

You don't have to worry about this tax if the transfer is a gift.

This tax, which is based on the sale price of the property, is collected by the county recorder when a deed is recorded. No documentary transfer tax is due unless the property is sold. For example, a gift (including a transfer to a revocable living trust) or a transfer pursuant to a court order is exempt from the tax.

The basic tax rate is 55¢ per $500 of the sales price. Some cities add surtaxes so that the total rate is considerably higher. For example, the total rate in San

Francisco is $5 per $1000. You can find out the rate in your city by calling the county recorder's office.

Other Local Transfer Taxes: A few cities (Berkeley, for example) impose an "anti-speculation" tax on sellers who have owned the property only a short time. Again, the county recorder's office can tell you if any extra local taxes will be imposed on your transfer.

6. Laws Penalizing Transfers Made to Defraud Creditors

If you think you may become insolvent (that is, have more debts than you can pay) and may have to declare bankruptcy, special rules may restrict your right to transfer or mortgage valuable property. If these rules apply, you must receive full value in return for any transfer. Put another way, if you give property away (put it in someone else's name) to frustrate the bankruptcy laws, the transfer may be considered fraudulent.[25] In some circumstances, the transfer can be voided by a court and the property used to pay your creditors.

In general, transfers immediately before bankruptcy are suspect, and transfers made up to a year before bankruptcy can be trouble. The point is if you are in bad financial shape and have been thinking about declaring bankruptcy, get advice from an experienced lawyer or accountant before you transfer property.

D. DO YOU NEED A TITLE SEARCH AND TITLE INSURANCE?

As discussed briefly above, title insurance is a way for a buyer (or lender financing a purchase) to be sure that if there's a problem with the title to the property he's just bought, the title insurance company will make it good. Insurance protects the buyer against problems that have already occurred. For example, suppose somebody once put the wrong property description on a deed, forged an owner's signature, forgot to get her spouse to sign the deed, or otherwise messed up. If for some reason a title search doesn't disclose the error, insurance will protect the buyer and lender. Title insurance doesn't protect against acts of the government such as condemnation proceedings or zoning restrictions.

---

[25]Uniform Fraudulent Transfer Act, Civil Code § 3439 et seq.

FAMILY FORGERY

Title insurance also protects buyers from the consequences of forged deeds. You may not think you need to check the title records of your property for forged documents, but forgeries by family members are on the rise, according to title insurance companies. A common scenario is forgery by a son or daughter who forges parents' names on a deed of trust making the property security for a loan. The child figures the parents may never find out about it if the loan is paid off and the child inherits the property anyway.

1. Title Searches

A title search turns up encumbrances on the title to property. If you don't know what encumbrances may exist on the property you want to transfer, and having this information is important (e.g., the property is going to new owners, or a significant sum is being paid for the transfer), you will definitely want to have a title search. If, on the other hand, you skipped the discussion of encumbrances (Section C.1 above) either because you know none exist or because your transfer involves a change of title (e.g., from tenancy in common to joint tenancy) but no new owners, you probably won't need a title search (though it never hurts).

A title search gives you an accurate picture of who owns the property and turns up most kinds of claims others may have against it. Specifically, a title search tells you if:

- the property has been pledged as security for a loan;
- an easement has been granted;

• certain liens[26] have been placed on the property;

• the property taxes haven't been paid;

• a lawsuit has been filed contesting ownership of the property; or

• a prior deed (say, the one transferring the property to whomever you got it from) was invalid.

A title search should check the validity of all prior transfers of the property. This string of transfers, which in California often stretches back in time to grants from the Mexican or United States government in the 19th century, is called the chain of title. If a deed to the land was ever improperly executed, or the property description in the deed was wrong, and the error went uncorrected, the current owner may not hold valid title to the land.[27]

These days, title insurance companies may not actually check all the old transfers. They rely on previous checks and just make sure there are no new problems with the title. Computerized records have largely replaced microfiche records, and the computer data often do not include the older transfers.

Virtually no layperson does a title search herself; it's a tedious, time-consuming job. And without some experience, it's easy to mess up. But if you want to be sure title to the property is clear, what should you do? Let's stop a minute and look at your options.

1. Go without a title search. This may not, depending on your circumstances, be as risky as it sounds. If you are merely changing the way title is held and not bringing in any new owners, or putting property in a revocable living trust, you may not need a title search.

Also, if the property was transferred to the current owner fairly recently, the title was checked then (as it always is in standard transfers; a bank wouldn't think of loaning money to finance the purchase of property without it), and you know that no liens or other encumbrances have been filed since, you're pretty safe not bothering with another search.

2. Get a "property profile" that checks the current title only. Title companies, which keep copies of the public records in their offices, furnish free "property profiles" that show the current state of the title to property (that is, without checking all the prior transfers, as a full title search would). Although they don't usually charge for the service, title companies probably expect to handle the escrow when you sell the property.

A property profile contains photocopies of everything in the public records that affects the property now. It typically includes:

---

[26]A lien is a legal hold on property that prevents title to the the property from being transferred until the lienholder (creditor) is paid the lien amount.

[27]Theoretically, all transfers are recorded in the public records. If evidence of a transfer—a link in the chain of title—is missing, that's a problem in itself, and it may necessitate a trip to court to resolve any uncertainty.

• Cover page: This lists the property address, owner, assessed value, and property tax due.

• Grant deed: A copy of the deed that transferred title to the current owner will always be included.

• Deeds of trust: All deeds of trust recorded against the property should be included. Make sure all pages of the deeds, including attachments, are there. Many property profiles only have the first page of the trust deed, which may not contain critical "due on sale" or "acceleration" clauses. The deed will not expressly tell you whether it is the first, second or third deed of trust recorded against the property; that is determined by the order in which they were recorded.

• Assessor's map: This shows the subdivision map filed with the county. The map shows the lots and boundaries of the property and also the assessor's parcel number (APN), which the assessor uses on the tax bills. It's critical that you check the legal description and APN given on your grant deed against what's on this map.

3. Pay a pro to do the title search. This is by far the most popular choice. For $100 to $250 or so, you can hire a title company to conduct a title search of your property. The fee is one of those "closing costs" that every buyer of real estate has come to know and love. The company will search the public records and issue a report showing:

• the legal owner's name;

• all liens, restrictions, easements, and other encumbrances;

• the legal description of the property; and

• local property taxes that have been assessed.

Some title companies do not sell title reports separately; you must also buy title insurance. The price of insurance depends on the value of the property; $1000 to $1500 for property worth $100,000 is a good estimate. You may need to make a few phone calls to find a company in your area that will do a title search separately.

COMPARISON SHOPPING MAY SAVE YOU MONEY
THIS TITLE INFORMATION HAS BEEN FURNISHED WITHOUT CHARGE BY
TITLE INSURANCE COMPANY

IN CONFORMANCE WITH THE RULES AND REGULATIONS ESTABLISHED BY THE
CALIFORNIA INSURANCE COMMISSIONER. WHO URGES YOU TO SHOP FOR THE
BEST SERVICE AVAILABLE AND COMPARE CHARGES AND FEES FOR TITLE
INSURANCE. ESCROW. AND OTHER SERVICES ASSOCIATED WITH THE
PURCHASE OR SALE OF A HOME.

PROPERTY PROFILE

ADDRESS: 5892 Eagle Creek Road

Richmond, California 94807

RECORD OWNER: REAL PROPERTIES, INC.

DEED   Recording date: **Sep.20,1984**   Documentary transfer tax: $ **22.55**

CONCURRENT TRUST DEED, IF ANY: (See attached)

LEGAL DESCRIPTION: (See attached deed copy and plat)

TAX INFORMATION:

Assessors Parcel No.	**527-012-002**
Assessed Value Land	$ **31,008**
Assessed Value Improvements	$ **19,992**
Exemption	$
Net Assessed Value	$ **51,000**
Installments	$ **359.33**
	$ **359.33**

HORTON FOO
CUSTOMER SERVICE
REPRESENTATIVE

XXX TITLE INSURANCE CO.
203 SOUTH OREGON STREET
WALNUT CREEK CA 95672
415-933-7920

In lieu of the above, see attached copy of Assessment Roll.

XXX TITLE INSURANCE

This information is furnished as a public service. Although care has been taken in its preparation.
the company assumes no liability for its accuracy or completeness.
Please note that concurrent trust deed information may not show all encumbrances of record.

CAA-298 W (Rev. 1-82)

WHEN RECORDED. PLEASE MAIL THIS
INSTRUMENT TO

DAVID MACLEAN
P.O. Box 1
Richmond, CA. 94801

84 137605

SEP 20 1984

Order No   49333
Escrow No   APN #527-012-002

RECORDED AT REQUEST OF
TITLE COMPANY
OF CONTRA COSTA

M_____Min Past___M.

OFFICIAL RECORDS OF
CONTRA COSTA COUNTY

COUNTY RECORDER

FEE $ 7.00

SPACE ABOVE FOR RECORDER'S USE ONLY

④

SHORT FORM DEED OF TRUST AND ASSIGNMENT OF RENTS

This Deed of Trust, made this   17   day of   September, 1984   , between

REAL PROPERTIES, INC. , a corporation

, herein called TRUSTOR,

whose address is   P.O. Box 682,   Berkeley CA 94702
                    (number and street)   (city)   (zone)   (state)

TITLE COMPANY OF CONTRA COSTA, a California corporation, herein called Trustee, and

DAVID MACLEAN

, herein called BENEFICIARY.

Witnesseth: That Trustor IRREVOCABLY GRANTS, TRANSFERS AND ASSIGNS to TRUSTEE IN TRUST, WITH
POWER OF SALE, that property in City of Richmond, Contra Costa County, California, described as:

FOR LEGAL DESCRIPTION SEE EXHIBIT "A" ATTACHED HERETO

FOR FURTHER TERMS AND CONDITIONS SEE EXHIBIT "B" ATTACHED HERETO

TOGETHER WITH the rents, issues and profits thereof, SUBJECT, HOWEVER, to the right, power and authority given to
and conferred upon Beneficiary by paragraph (10) of the provisions incorporated herein by reference to collect and apply
such rents, issues and profits.
For the Purpose of Securing: 1 Performance of each agreement of Trustor incorporated by reference or contained
herein 2 Payment of the indebtedness evidenced by one promissory note of even date herewith, and any extension or renewal
thereof, in the principal sum of $ 18,129.72 ——executed by Trustor in favor of Beneficiary or order. 3. Payment of
such further sums as the then record owner of said property hereafter may borrow from Beneficiary, when evidenced by
another note (or notes) reciting it is so secured.
To Protect the Security of This Deed of Trust, Trustor Agrees: By the execution and delivery of this Deed
of Trust and the Note secured hereby, that provisions (1) to (14), inclusive, (which provisions are printed on the reverse
hereof of the fictitious Deed of Trust recorded in the office of the County Recorder of each of the following counties in the
State of California on July 3, 1968, in the Book and at the Page designated after the name of each County, which provisions
are identical in each Deed of Trust, shall be and they are hereby incorporated herein and made an integral part hereof for
all purposes as though set forth herein at length.

COUNTY	REEL OR BOOK	IMAGE OR PAGE	COUNTY	REEL OR BOOK	IMAGE OR PAGE	COUNTY	REEL OR BOOK	IMAGE OR PAGE
Alameda	2210	970	San Francisco	B-254	678	Santa Cruz	1890	217
Marin	2223	30	San Joaquin	3221	325	San Mateo	5497	162
Monterey	563	919	Sonoma	2339	251	Santa Clara	8178	33
Napa	769	977	Stanislaus	2227	312	Contra Costa	5660	126
Sacramento	68 07-03	250	Solano	1515	107	El Dorado	1443	10

The undersigned Trustor requests that a copy of any Notice of Default and of any Notice of Sale hereunder be mailed
to him at his address hereinbefore set forth

STATE OF CALIFORNIA
COUNTY OF

On September 19,   198_
before me, the undersigned, a Notary Public in and for said County
and State personally appeared Diane A. Holst

_____ to be the
James B. Holst   President and
_____ to me to be the   Secretary of
the corporation that executed the within instrument and known to
me to be the persons who executed the within instrument on behalf
of the corporation therein named, and acknowledged to me that such
corporation executed the same, and acknowledged to me that such
corporation executed the within instrument pursuant to its by-laws
or a resolution of its board of directors
WITNESS my hand and official seal

OFFICIAL SEAL
CASSY PEAR
NOTARY PUBLIC CALIFORNIA
CONTRA COSTA COUNTY
My Commission Expires Nov 14, 1987

Cassy Pear
Notary Public in and for said County and State

Cassy Pear

REAL PROPERTIES, INC., a corporation

BY Diane Holst, President

BY James Holst, Secretary

RECORD ONLY IN COUNTIES LISTED ABOVE   C 10

RECORDING REQUESTED BY

TITLE COMPANY

AND WHEN RECORDED MAIL TO

REAL PROPERTIES, INC.
P.O. Box 682
Berkeley CA 94702

SEP 20 1984

84 137602

RECORDED AT REQUEST OF

BOOK 11983 PAGE 202

TITLE COMPANY
OF CONTRA COSTA

M ___8___ Min. Past ___4___ M

OFFICIAL RECORDS OF
CONTRA COSTA COUNTY

COUNTY RECORDER

CONTRA COSTA CO
TRANSFER TAX
$ 22.55

SURVEY
MONUMENT
FUND
$10

SPACE ABOVE FOR RECORDER'S USE ONLY

MAIL TAX STATEMENTS TO
NO CHANGE

COUNTY MONUMENT USER FEE $10.00

DOCUMENTARY TRANSFER TAX $ 22.55

COMPUTED ON FULL VALUE OF
PROPERTY CONVEYED, OR
COMPUTED ON FULL VALUE LESS
LIENS & ENCUMBRANCES REMAINING
ING THEREON AT TIME OF SALE

AS DECLARED BY THE UNDERSIGNED

Signature of declarant or agent determining tax

A P N.   527-012-002
         49333
Order No
Escrow No

GRANT DEED

/ DAVID MACLEAN, an unmarried man

(GRANTOR - GRANTORS)

FOR A VALUABLE CONSIDERATION, receipt of which is hereby acknowledged,
Do es Hereby Grant To

REAL PROPERTIES, INC., a corporation

the real property in the   City of Richmond
County of   Contra Costa   , State of California, described as follows

FOR LEGAL DESCRIPTION SEE EXHIBIT "A" ATTACHED HERETO

Dated   9/17/84

STATE OF CALIFORNIA
COUNTY OF   } SS
CONTRA COSTA

On ____ September 19 , 1984
before me, the undersigned, a Notary Public in and for said
County and State, personally appeared ____
David Maclean

known to me (or proved to me on the basis of satisfactory
evidence) to be the same person whose name __is__

subscribed to the within instrument, and acknowledged to
me that ____he____ executed the same
WITNESS my hand and official seal

Notary's signature   Cassy Pear

David Maclean

FOR NOTARY STAMP OR SEAL

OFFICIAL SEAL
CASSY PEAR
NOTARY PUBLIC CALIFORNIA
CONTRA COSTA COUNTY
My Commission Expires May 26, 1987

CCPN

Order No 49333 PC

BOOK 11983 PAGE 208

EXHIBIT "A" as referred to in the deed of trust dated 9/17/84 REAL PROPERTIES, INC., to trustee an ' David McLean beneficiary

The land referred to in this Report is situated in the State of California, County of Contra Costa City of Richmond and is described as follows:

Portion of Lots 11 and 13, Block 19, map of the San Pablo Villa Tract, filed September 21, 1905, Map Book C, page 65, Contra Costa County Records, described as follows:

Beginning on the east line of Hayes Street, formerly Powell Street, distant thereon north 0 degrees 45' west 59 feet from the southwest corner of said Block 19; thence from said point of beginning north 0 degrees 45' east along the east line of Hayes Street 41.5 feet; thence southeasterly parallel with the south line of Emeric Avenue, formerly Clay Street 112.5 feet to the west line of Lot 12; thence southerly along said line 41.5 feet; thence northwesterly parallel with the south line of Emeric Avenue 112.5 feet to the point of beginning.

SCHEDULE A
CLTA Preliminary Report
1-1-84

Page 2 of 2

TITLE
GUARANTY COMPANY

Order No. 49333 PC

EXHIBIT "A" AS REFERRED TO IN THE DEED FROM DAVID MACLEAN TO REAL PROPERTIES, INC., a California corporation dated 9/17/84

The land referred to in this Report is situated in the State of California, County of Contra Costa and is described as follows:

City of Richmond

Portion of Lots 11 and 13, Block 19, map of the San Pablo Villa Tract, filed September 21, 1905, Map Book C, page 65, Contra Costa County Records, described as follows:

Beginning on the east line of Hayes Street, formerly Powell Street, distant thereon north 0 degrees 45' west 59 feet from the southwest corner of said Block 19; thence from said point of beginning north 0 degrees 45' east along the east line of Hayes Street 41.5 feet; thence southeasterly parallel with the south line of Emeric Avenue, formerly Clay Street 112.5 feet to the west line of Lot 12; thence southerly along said line 41.5 feet; thence northwesterly parallel with the south line of Emeric Avenue 112.5 feet to the point of beginning.

BOOK 11983 PAGE 203

84 137602

END OF DOCUMENT

SCHEDULE A
CLTA Preliminary Report
1-1-84

Page 2 of 2

TITLE
GUARANTY COMPANY

3∞11983r.209

"Exhibit A to Deed of Trust

~~This Note shall... ...failure to make such periodic payments shall not be a default of this Note. Unpaid payments shall be applied to principal and shall accumulate and be paid in full with the final payment of the Note.~~

Payor has the option of making a prepayment of several monthly installments (minimum six installments). By doing so, the payor may discount the total sum of the actual payments by __10__ per cent and the resulting amount be paid in lieu of the total sum of the actual scheduled installment payments due for that period. Said prepayment shall waive installment payments for the same number of months after the payments were prepaid. This Note to have no prepayment penalty if paid in full or in part before the due date. Payor may at any time within __60__ months of the date of this Note prepay the entire Note and may discount the then due principal balance by __10__ per cent.

At the time this Note is due and payable, Note Holder agrees to extend the due date for an additional twelve months, if payor agrees to change the interest rate to 2% over the Federal Discount Rate.

~~The Note Holder agrees to...~~

~~The Note Holder agrees to subordinate this Note and Deed of Trust to any new financing...~~

Should the Note Holder decide to sell this Note, the Note Holder must first offer it to the payor. The payor may purchase it within 30 days. The payor shall also have 30 days to match any bona fide written offer received at a later time from a third party.

The obligation for the payment of this Note and Deed of Trust can be assumed by another party at any time in the future retaining the same terms and conditions.

The liability of this Note shall be limited to the property itself, and shall not extend beyond it. The payor shall have no personal liability. This Note is given as a portion of the purchase price of real property and any Note Holder thereof shall accept the Note subject to any and all claims arising out of the purchase transaction.

IAS Form 101-B Revision 9.13 Copyright 1984

END OF DOCUMENT

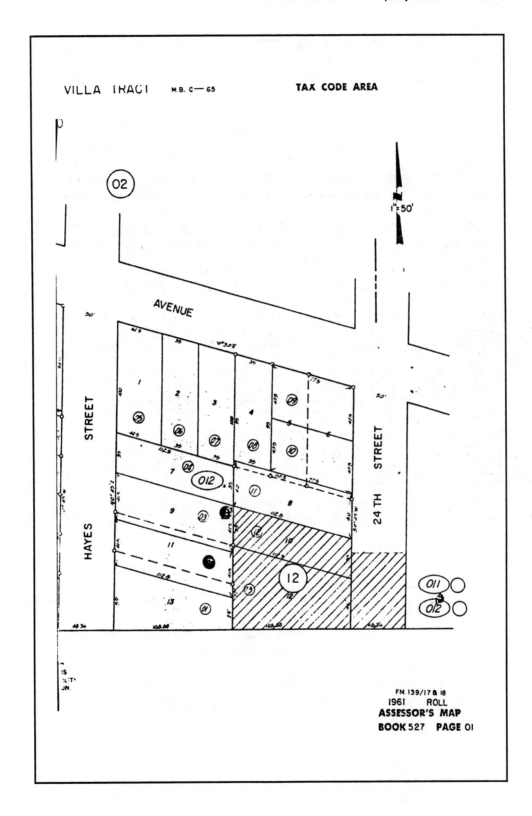

VILLA TRACT   M.B. C—65   TAX CODE AREA

1"=50'

ASSESSOR'S MAP
BOOK 527   PAGE 01

FN.139/17 & 18
1961   ROLL

4. Do the search yourself. If you're a diehard do-it-yourselfer, and you have plenty of spare time, you can try to do the search yourself, but we don't recommend it. It's just not a cost-effective way to spend your time. (And a title company won't insure a title that it hasn't checked itself.)

To search the title to property you must start with the "Grantor-Grantee Index" (usually kept on microfiche) at the county recorder's office. In it you can look up the current owner's name and start going backwards in time from the current deed. Remember that you have a long, long way to go (more than 100 years, almost certainly), and that you'll need to check every name and legal description in every deed to the property. You will also need to look up the property in the county assessor's property tax records and the general county records that show bankruptcies, divorces, name changes, and judgments. Finally, you will need to go through the bankruptcy records of the federal district court.

It should be apparent to you why we recommend that you don't do a title search yourself. It's a complex task that takes practice to get good (or even competent) at, and given the risks involved, it's well worth it to pay a professional. Moreover, when you go to sell (or borrow money on) the land later, no one will want to rely on an amateur's title search, so you'll probably end up paying for a title search sometime. For your peace of mind, if you want a title search, get it done right.

What a title search can't show. Obviously, a title search can't uncover unrecorded transfers. And no title search will reveal the extent to which California's community (marital) property laws affect ownership of the property. Those laws may mean, for example, that even if the house is in one spouse's name alone it belongs to both and that both must sign the deed. We discuss this point, and how to handle it, in Chapter 3, Section A.

Similarly, the California Supreme Court's "palimony" decision in *Marvin v. Marvin* may mean that an unmarried live-in lover may have property rights based on an implied contract. See Chapter 3, Section B.

2. Title Insurance

Usually, the point of having a title search is to enable you to buy title insurance. It works like this: the title insurance company searches the public records and issues a "preliminary title report" (the "prelim"), which shows all encumbrances of record. Then the company issues a title insurance policy, guaranteeing that the title is clear of encumbrances except those specified on the preliminary report.

ABC Title Company

☐ 1240 10th Street, San Rafael CA 94901
Telephone: (415) 457-9245

☐ 40 "B" Street, San Francisco CA 94103 4947
Telephone: (415) 339-9245

PRELIMINARY REPORT

Issued for the sole use of:

Coldwell Banker
500 Sir Francis Drake Boulevard
Greenbrae, California
Attn: Julie

Our Order No.   355-728

Reference

When Replying Please Contact:

Jesse Costa
454-8209

Property Address: 13 Bretano Way, Greenbrae, California

In response to the above referenced application for a policy of title insurance,   Title Company hereby reports that it
is prepared to issue, or cause to be issued, as of the date hereof, a Policy or Policies of Title Insurance describing the land
and the estate or interest therein hereinafter set forth, insuring against loss which may be sustained by reason of any
defect, lien or encumbrance not shown or referred to as an Exception below or not excluded from coverage pursuant to the
printed Schedules, Conditions and Stipulations of said policy forms.

The printed Exceptions and Exclusions from the coverage of said Policy or Policies are set forth in Schedule I and Schedule
I (continued) attached. Copies of the Policy forms should be read. They are available from the office which issued this
report.

This report (and any supplements or amendments hereto) is issued solely for the purpose of facilitating the issuance of a
policy of title insurance and no liability is assumed hereby. If it is desired that liability be assumed prior to the issuance of a
policy of title insurance, a Binder or Commitment should be requested.

Dated as of _____May 15_____ , 19 84 , at 7:30 A.M.

TITLE COMPANY

Title Officer

Jean Tufton

The form of policy of title insurance contemplated by this report is:

"an American Land Title Association Loan Policy - 1970, loan
policy; a California Land Title Association Standard Coverage
policy - 1973, owner's policy."

The estate or interest in the land hereinafter described or referred to covered by this Report is: a fee

Title to said estate or interest at the date hereof is vested in:

JOHN O'HUFFELL and CLAUDIA O'HUFFELL, his wife, as
Co-Trustees under that certain Declaration of Trust,
executed November 18, 1975

Page _____ of _____ Pages

ORDER NO.

The land referred to in this Report is situated in the State of California, County of Marin
and is described as follows:

LOT 195, as shown upon that certain map entitled, "Map of Greenbrae Sub.
No. One, Marin Co. Calif.", filed May 2, 1946 in Book 6 of Maps, at Page
7, Marin County Records.

At the date hereof exceptions to coverage in addition to the Exceptions and Exclusions in said policy form would be as
follows:

1. Taxes, general and special, for the fiscal year 1984&85, a lien
not yet due or payable.

2. The lien of Supplemental Taxes assessed pursuant to Chapter 498,
Statutes of 1983 of the State of California.

3. Taxes, general and special, for the fiscal year 1983&84, as follows:

Assessor's Parcel No.: 70-192-11
Code No.   : 68-004

1st Installment   : $371.19 Paid
2nd Installment   : $371.19 Delinquent
                       37.11 Penalty
Land   : $24,960
Improvement Value   : $40,210
Personal Prop. Value : $NONE
Exemption   : $7000 - Householder

"Any amounts which may be added to the Property Tax amounts by reason of
a Reappraisal of any improvements added to, or change of Ownership of,
the herein described Premises subsequent to March 1, 1975".

Page _____ of _____ Pages

The buyer's policy is in the amount of the purchase price of the property. Usually it is a CLTA (California Land Title Association) policy. If someone (including the seller) is lending money to the buyer, and the loan is secured by a deed of trust on the property, the lender usually buys a separate insurance policy that covers him for the amount of the loan. The lender's policy is often an ALTA (American Land Title Association) policy, which offers broader coverage than the standard CLTA policy.

3. What If the Title Search Turns Up Problems?

If there is a problem in the chain of title—meaning that somewhere along the line the property was imperfectly transferred—the current owners will have to correct the defect. Correction will entail either a new deed (often in the form of a quitclaim deed, discussed in Chapter 6) or going to court to have a judge resolve any uncertainty in who owns what.

For example, say that your father, the previous owner of the property you want to transfer, mistakenly left out a 50-foot strip of the property when he deeded the land to you. If this mistake is not corrected, the new owners will be getting less than they think they are.

What can be done to rectify the mistake? Your father can execute a new deed transferring his interest in the omitted property to you. If he were no longer living, you would have to go to court in the county where the property is located and get a judgment saying the property belongs to you. That process almost certainly requires a lawyer and is beyond the scope of this book.

E. CHECKLIST

Here is a checklist that you can refer to as you go through the book:

CHECKLIST FOR REAL PROPERTY TRANSFERS

Current owner must:	New owner must:
Determine who must sign the deed	Decide whether or not to buy title insurance
If there are existing loans, check with lender to see if balance will become due when property sold	Order title search, if necessary
	Decide how to take title
Make disclosures about condition of property, if required by statute	
Fill out and sign correct deed form	
Have signatures on the deed notarized	
Deliver deed to new owner	Record deed with county recorder's office, pay transfer tax if applicable, and file Preliminary Change in Ownership Report with county recorder
File federal gift tax return, if necessary	File Change In Ownership Statement with county assessor, if required

C H A P T E R 3

WHO MUST SIGN THE DEED?

One important question you must answer before you transfer title to real property is whether you can do it by yourself or whether you need someone else's cooperation. The basic rule is simple: if someone else appears to have, for any legitimate reason, a claim to an ownership interest in the property being transferred, you should not try to transfer title unless he either gives up that claim (by signing a quitclaim deed to you) or signs the transfer deed along with you. Otherwise, your transfer will be incomplete—you can only transfer what you own.

The same rules apply when you want to use a trust deed to make the property security for repayment of a debt (Chapter 5), or when you want to transfer property to a living trust, or when you just want to change the way title is held without changing who owns the property (Chapter 4). If all the property owners don't sign, you won't accomplish your goal.

The consequences of an incomplete or confused transfer are unhappy. First of all, the person receiving the property gets less than appears in the transfer deed. And when the deed recognizing the botched or incomplete transfer is recorded, the public record of ownership will be wrong. This can make it difficult, later, to sell the property or borrow money on it. Enough said, we hope. The point is that you want to be sure about who owns the property being transferred and that each owner signs the deed.

Exceptions, exceptions: Like almost all good advice, our admonition to have all owners sign the deed doesn't always apply. In a few instances it may make sense for you to transfer your part interest in real property, if whomever you're transferring it to clearly understands that you have only a part interest in it. For example, if you own land with two siblings, you may want to go ahead and transfer your interest to your brother and let him deal with your sister about getting her to make a similar transfer.

Before you get into the mechanics of figuring out when you need to get someone else to participate in the transfer of a piece of real property, take a look to see if you are in one of the four common situations outlined just below.

1. If you are married, both you and your spouse are willing to sign the deed, and there are no other co-owners.

2. If you are single, not living with anyone, and are the sole owner of the property (you are the only one who needs to sign the deed).

3. If all co-owners of the property agree to the transfer or the change in the way title is held (e.g., from tenancy in common to joint tenancy) and all will sign the deed (with their spouses, if any are married).

4. If the property is owned in the name of a partnership, and all partners are willing to sign the deed.

If you are in one of these categories, you can safely transfer your property by yourself and skip the rest of this chapter. This means if you want to sell or give away property, or put it in a living trust, you can go directly to Chapter 4. If you want to make property security for a loan and execute a trust deed, go to Chapter 5 instead. If you don't fit in one of these four categories, it means you need more information before you make your transfer. Here is a short outline of how to proceed:

• if you are married or living with someone who won't consent to the transfer you want to make, read Section A below.

• if you are an unmarried co-owner of property, and the other co-owners don't want to make the transfer, go to Section B.

• if you are acting as a trustee for a minor or someone else who owns property, go to Section C.

• if you want to transfer partnership property, go to Section D.

• if someone must act for a property owner because he is a minor or incompetent (incapable of understanding or signing a deed), see Section E.

A. TRANSFERS FROM MARRIED PERSONS

The basic rule of transfers from married persons is that both spouses must sign the deed. Whether the property is in both names (held as community property, joint tenancy, or tenancy in common) or only in the name of one spouse, both should sign.[1]

The same is true if one spouse is a co-owner with other persons; spouses of all co-owners should sign. For example, if two brothers, Phillip and Charles, want to transfer some land they own together, both Phillip and Charles and their wives should sign the deed.

It's easy to understand why you need the signature of both spouses if both names are on the existing deed. But why do you need two signatures if the property is in one spouse's name and belongs to him as separate property? The answer lies in California's community property laws. California law regards most property acquired by a married person as community property—that is, it belongs to the spouses as a unit, not to either spouse separately. Both spouses must jointly make any transfer or encumbrance of community real property.[2] And because separate property owned by one spouse can easily be turned (at least partially) into community property (very easily if, for example, community property funds are used to improve it, pay taxes on it, or make payments on a mortgage), in practice both spouses must usually sign before any real property owned by a married person can be transferred or mortgaged.

The point, and it's an important one, is that there's usually no reliable way for a third party to know whether under the law a married person really owns a piece of real property all by himself. For that reason, banks and escrow companies always insist that both spouses sign deeds and other documents involved in property transfers. Having both spouses sign the deed instantly and easily eliminates any doubts about the completeness of the transfer, and no one has to worry about whether or not the property was separate or community.

Remember that even if a bank or title insurer isn't involved in the current transfer, one or both will almost certainly be in on some subsequent sale and will insist on a title search then. If it is found that a prior transfer was made by one spouse without the signature of the other, the bank, or a title insurance company the bank depends on, may not approve the new proposed transfer.

---

[1]It may be more convenient (because of distance or timing) for your spouse to sign a separate quitclaim deed to you, releasing whatever interest he may have in the property. Then you can go ahead and sign a grant deed (transferring the property to someone else) or a trust deed (making the property security for a loan) yourself.

[2]Civil Code § 5127. Transfers made by one spouse, if title is held in the name of that spouse only, may be challenged in court for up to a year after the deed is recorded in the county recorder's office.

WHAT ABOUT LIVING TOGETHER?

In a few instances, you may need the signature of the person you live with even if you aren't married. Since the California Supreme Court's 1976 decision in the Lee Marvin-Michele Triola Marvin "palimony" case, it's possible that a "significant other" may have a claim to property you acquire while living together.

In the Marvin case, the court found that the couple had an implied contract (that is, a mutual understanding that wasn't explicitly stated or written down) to share property ownership. Because California courts now recognize such implied contracts, if they can be proved, some members of unmarried couples undoubtedly have ownership interests in the property held in the names of their friends (or ex-friends). If you think your friend may sometime press a claim against property you want to transfer, play it safe. Talk the situation over. If you reach an amicable understanding, get a quitclaim deed from him before the transfer.

What if you are married but something prevents your spouse from joining in the transfer of title to property that you are convinced is yours alone? The transfer can still safely be made without the signature of your spouse if you are sure that the property is your separate property and others would readily draw the same conclusion. To make this determination, you must take the time to become familiar with California community property laws. Here are some rules of thumb.

In general, real estate is probably all or partially community property if:

• the property was acquired during the marriage with money earned by either spouse after marriage; or

• both your names appear on the deed; or

• your spouse has contributed a significant amount of time or labor to the property's improvement; or

• community funds[3] were used for improvements, taxes, or mortgage payments.

In a few instances, however, property belongs entirely to one spouse alone (separate property) and can be transferred without the other spouse's consent. To be separate property, the real estate must pass two tests. First, it must have been:

• owned and paid for by one spouse before the marriage; or

• given to one spouse as a gift; or

• inherited by one spouse; or

• paid for totally with one spouse's separate property; or

• acquired after the spouses permanently separated.

Second, no community property funds can have been spent on improvements, taxes, or mortgage payments for the property.

If, for example, you purchased the property with your separate property money, you never used your earnings or other community funds to make improvements or pay the mortgage or taxes, and title is held in your name alone, it will qualify as your separate property. If so, you can legally transfer it without your spouse's signature. To repeat an important point, if a bank or escrow company is involved, it will probably be conservative on this point and insist on your spouse's signature no matter how persuasively you argue that your real estate isn't community property.

If after reading this you are sure the real estate is your separate property, and there is some problem with obtaining your spouse's signature, you can go ahead and transfer title to the property with only your signature on the deed. But again, remember that there may be problems down the road when the new owner goes to transfer title, because it may not be clear to a third party that your spouse had no claim to the property.

---

[3]Community funds are, in general, any funds acquired by either spouse during the marriage except those acquired by one spouse only by gift or inheritance.

B. TRANSFERS FROM UNMARRIED CO-OWNERS

We've divided this chapter along marriage lines because of the enormous importance of California's marital (community) property laws any time you transfer real property. This section deals only with transactions where all owners who want to transfer property are unmarried.

If all co-owners of the property agree to the transfer or the change in the way title is held (e.g., from tenancy in common to joint tenancy) and all will sign the deed (with their spouses, if any are married), you can go directly to Chapter 4, which discusses how the new owners should take title. If a co-owner wants to transfer his interest on his own, read on.

To know your rights when you are a co-owner of real property, you must know in what form you hold title. You are either a "joint tenant," a "tenant in common," or a partner.[4]

To find out how you and your co-owners hold title, consult the deed that gave you title to the property. It will probably specify that you and your co-owners hold title either "as joint tenants," "as tenants in common," or in the name of the partnership. If it doesn't say, you are tenants in common, unless the property was bought with partnership funds (in which case the partnership owns the property).[5]

Joint tenancy is also sometimes indicated by the form "to John and Claudia with right of survivorship." Title documents for personal property such as stocks, cars, and bank accounts often create a joint tenancy by simply linking the names of joint owners with "or," but this form is virtually never used for real property. Given that circumstance, and the general rule that if the type of title isn't specified, a tenancy in common is created, a deed that merely joins the names of the new owners with "or" could be considered ambiguous. To clarify the situation, you and the other co-owners should execute a new deed to yourselves, spelling out how you want to hold title, before transferring title to anyone else.

---

[4]Legal terminology note: although co-owners are referred to as "tenants" (i.e., "tenants in common" or "joint tenants"), this doesn't mean they're renting the property. It's just another archaic legal term that, unfortunately, is impossible to avoid.

[5]If you received your interest in the land from someone who was a part-owner (someone who didn't own the whole property), you are a tenant in common. Thus if your deed transferred to you "a half interest in the following property . . ." you are a tenant in common.

Recording requested by
John and Claudia O'Huffell
78 Sherwood Drive
Oakland, CA 94618

and when recorded mail
this deed and tax statements to:

same as above

For recorder's use

GRANT DEED

☒ This transfer is exempt from the documentary transfer tax.
☐ The documentary transfer tax is $_____ and is computed on
    ☐ the full value of the interest or property conveyed.
    ☐ the full value less the value of liens or encumbrances remaining thereon at the time of sale.
The property is located in ☐ an unincorporated area. ☒ the city of ___Oakland_____.

For a valuable consideration, receipt of which is hereby acknowledged,
    JOHN O'HUFFELL or CLAUDIA O'HUFFELL

hereby grant(s) to
    JOHN O'HUFFELL and CLAUDIA O'HUFFELL, as joint tenants,

the following real property in the City of __Oakland_____, County of __Alameda_____,
California:

1. Tenants in Common

As an unmarried tenant in common, you are free to do just about whatever you want with your interest in commonly owned property. If you want to get rid of your interest, you may sell it, give it away, or leave it in your will, just like any other property you own alone.

a. Transferring Part Interests

Because tenants in common own "undivided interests" in the property, each can only sell that interest, not a specific part of the property. If, for example,

Joanne and her brother Ed own half interests in a 10-acre piece of property as tenants in common, Joanne is free to sell her interest in the property to her friend Jillian. Ed can't stop her.[6] Only Joanne needs to sign the deed.

Joanne, however, cannot sell five acres of the land; she can only transfer her half-interest in the whole property. That's what her friend Jillian would get: a half-interest in the entire 10 acres.

b. Partitions

If, as is usually the case, a co-owner doesn't want to transfer an undivided interest, and the other co-owners won't agree to execute deeds splitting the property,[7] he may request that a court in the county where the land is located either split the property or order it sold and the proceeds split. That process is called a partition.

Every tenant has an absolute right to obtain a partition of the property. No particular reason is necessary. The court usually orders that the property be sold and the proceeds divided among the co-tenants according to their ownership interests. The court can, however, order that the property be physically divided. How to file a partition action is beyond the scope of this book; a lawyer's advice will be needed.

2. Joint Tenants

If you hold title to real property in joint tenancy (discussed in Chapter 4, Section B), you probably know that the most important characteristic of that way of holding title is that upon a joint tenant's death, his interest in the property goes to the surviving joint tenants. Nevertheless, you can easily transfer your interest in jointly held property, whether or not the other joint tenants agree to or even know of the change. We discuss how below.

---

[6]Jillian and Ed would be the new tenants in common, and Jillian would own an undivided interest in the whole property. See Chapter 4, Section A if you're interested in a discussion of the features of tenancy in common.

[7]If co-owners want to split up the property, they need to execute two deeds, each transferring half the property. Remember that zoning laws often restrict how property may be divided. Check with your city or county planning department before you start carving up your land. If the property is on the coast, you probably also need approval from the California Coastal Commission.

a. Transferring Your Interest in the Property

The simplest way for a joint tenant to end the joint tenancy is to execute and record a deed transferring his interest to himself, or anyone else, as a tenant in common. That destroys the joint tenancy as to his interest.[8] To transfer his interest in the property (now held as a tenancy in common), the joint tenant need only sign the deed himself.

Example: Jesse and Angie own their house as joint tenants. Without telling Angie, Jesse executes a deed transferring his interest from himself as a joint tenant to himself as a tenant in common.

Recording requested by

Jesse M. Costa
937 Livermore Ave.
Danville, CA 94558

and when recorded mail
this deed and tax statements to:

same as above

For recorder's use

GRANT DEED

☒ This transfer is exempt from the documentary transfer tax.
☐ The documentary transfer tax is $_____ and is computed on
　　☐ the full value of the interest or property conveyed.
　　☐ the full value less the value of liens or encumbrances remaining thereon at the time of sale.
The property is located in ☐ an unincorporated area. ☒ the city of _Danville_____.

For a valuable consideration, receipt of which is hereby acknowledged,
　　　　JESSE M. COSTA, joint tenant,

hereby grant(s) to
　　　　JESSE M. COSTA, as a tenant in common,

　　　　a one-half interest in
the following real property in the City of __Danville_____, County of _Contra Costa_,
California:

---

[8]If a deed severing the joint tenancy is executed by only one joint tenant, it usually must be recorded (filed in the county recorder's office; see Chapter 7) before that joint tenant's death to defeat the survivorship interests of the remaining joint tenants. See Chapter 7, Section B.

This severs the joint tenancy, as long as the deed is recorded before Jesse's death. Jesse and Angie become tenants in common. Upon either's death, his or her half-interest will pass to beneficiaries under a will or heirs,[9] not to the surviving joint tenant (again, the characteristics of joint tenancy are set out in detail in Chapter 4, Section B).

Suppose now that there are more than two joint tenants. If one executes a deed to herself as a tenant in common, she will then be a tenant in common with the other two co-tenants, who remain joint tenants with respect to their two-thirds interest in the property. Joint tenancy rules govern the relationship between the two joint tenants, while tenancy in common rules apply to relations between the joint tenants and the tenant in common.

Example: Marsha, Joe and Helen own a piece of property as joint tenants. Marsha sells her one-third interest to Dan. Dan does not become a joint tenant. He is a tenant in common with Joe and Helen. He is free to leave his interest in the property through his will (or put it into a living trust); if he doesn't have a will (or trust), it will pass to his heirs under state law. Joe and Helen are not entitled to receive it when Dan dies, and Dan will not receive their interests when they die. Joe and Helen, however, remain joint tenants as between themselves.

b. Getting the Property Partitioned

A joint tenant also has the right to obtain a court-ordered partition (division or sale) of the property. Partitions are discussed in subsection 1 just above.

c. Executing a Deed of Trust

A joint tenant may sign a deed of trust herself, making her interest in the property security for a loan. This does *not* terminate the joint tenancy. However, if a creditor forecloses on the property and a joint tenant's interest is sold, the sale terminates the joint tenancy (as between the buyer of the interest and the other joint tenant(s)) in the same way as a voluntary transfer would.

d. Transfers by Surviving Joint Tenants

We mentioned that a joint tenant's interest in property passes to the surviving joint tenants, who record an affidavit with the county recorder giving notice of the joint tenant's death.[10] If, later on, the surviving joint tenants want to transfer title to the property, they should sign the deed as "surviving joint tenants."

---

[9]If neither had a will, the property would pass under state "intestate succession" laws.

[10]The procedure is set out in Julia Nissley's *How to Probate an Estate* (Nolo Press).

C. TRANSFERS FROM TRUSTEES

Trusts are designed to hold property (in the name of a trustee) for someone (the beneficiary) for a certain period of time. It's common, for example, to put property in trust for a child.

As discussed in Chapter 4, Section F, property must be formally transferred, with a grant deed, to the trust. When the time comes to the transfer the property from the trust back to an outright owner (either the person who set up the trust, if the trust is being revoked, or the named beneficiary), another formal transfer, with a deed, is necessary. The trustee must sign the deed, which would look like this:

Recording requested by

David R. Maclean
665 Newman Street
St. Helena, CA 94573

and when recorded mail
this deed and tax statements to:

same as above

For recorder's use

GRANT DEED

☒This transfer is exempt from the documentary transfer tax.
☐The documentary transfer tax is $_____ and is computed on
    ☐the full value of the interest or property conveyed.
    ☐the full value less the value of liens or encumbrances remaining thereon at the time of sale.
The property is located in ☐an unincorporated area.☒the city of ___St. Helena___.

For a valuable consideration, receipt of which is hereby acknowledged,

      MARJORIE SIMMONS, TRUSTEE of the David R. Maclean trust,

hereby grant(s) to

      DAVID R. MACLEAN

the following real property in the City of __St. Helena__, County of __Napa__, California:

D. TRANSFERS OF PARTNERSHIP PROPERTY

Real property is often held in the name of a partnership, an entity formed by two or more people to conduct a business. The transfer rules are governed by the partnership agreement or, if the agreement doesn't cover it, the Uniform Partnership Act (UPA).[11] Under the UPA, any partner may transfer real property held in the partnership name if the transfer is apparently for carrying on the business of the partnership, unless

• the partner in fact doesn't have authority to make the particular transfer and

• the person with whom the partner deals knows the partner doesn't have the authority.

If the partnership agreement limits certain partners' authority to transfer real property, the partnership should record the agreement in any county where the partnership owns real property. Once it's recorded, it gives notice to all prospective purchasers that only certain partners can transfer partnership real property. Check the partnership agreement for restrictions and rules about how the transfer can be made.[12]

Example 1: Brian and Fred run a real estate business as partners. Their partnership agreement doesn't say anything about transferring the partnership's property. Under the UPA, either may sign a deed to transfer partnership property or subject it to a deed of trust.

Example 2: Fred wants to borrow money because he sunk all his savings in the partnership. He wants to sign a deed of trust giving the partnership's real property as security for a loan. Under the UPA (and most partnership agreements), he can't unless Brian agrees and signs, too, because this isn't in the course of partnership business.

Further, most partnership agreements restrict a partner's freedom to transfer only his interest in the partnership property. Usually, the other partners get a chance to buy out his interest before the partner is allowed to sell his interest in property freely.

Example: Jane decides she wants out of the partnership she, Jeremy and Ruth have, and decides to try to sell her interest in the partnership's real property. Under the terms of the partnership agreement, she must first offer to sell her interest to Ruth and Jeremy.

---

[11]Calif. Corporations Code § 15001 et seq.

[12]For a thorough discussion of partnership agreements, see *The Partnership Book*, by Clifford and Warner (Nolo Press).

E. TRANSFERS OF CORPORATE PROPERTY

Like partnerships, corporations are governed by special rules about how real property transfers can be made and who is authorized to make them. Generally, the board of directors must approve, by resolution, sale of corporate assets. The deed is signed by an officer of the corporation who is authorized by the board to sell property, and the corporate seal is embossed on the deed. If a transfer is made to liquidate the corporation's assets (not in the course of the corporation's business), shareholder approval may be required. Before you transfer corporate property, check the California Corporations Code.[13]

F. OWNERS WHO CAN'T SIGN A DEED

Not everyone who owns real property is free to transfer it. In certain narrow circumstances, a property owner may lack the legal capacity to execute a deed, and someone with proper legal standing must sign for the actual owner. The two most common situations are when a minor owns property or a property owner is mentally incompetent.

_____

[13]Also see *How to Form Your Own California Corporation*, by Tony Mancuso (Nolo Press), which contains information and forms necessary to form and run a small California corporation.

1. Minors

A minor (in California, someone less than 18 years old) may not make a valid deed. Any deed signed by a minor is void and has no effect. The minor's guardian (in most cases, someone approved by the probate court, because minors usually acquire real property by inheritance) must sign the deed.

The one exception is a minor who is emancipated—that is, one who has been married, is in the military, or who has received a decree of emancipation from a court.[14] An emancipated minor has the same rights as an adult when it comes to owning property.

2. Persons With Mental Impairment

All that is required of a person executing a deed, as far as mental capacity is concerned, is the ability to understand the nature of the transaction and its consequences. Old age, ill health, or some mental impairment does not automatically render a deed suspect.

If, however, a court has determined (in a competency hearing) that someone is of unsound mind, that person may not transfer property. Any deed signed by such a person is void. Although it is uncommon, a court can also invalidate a deed if it rules, after the fact, that the person was "entirely without understanding" when he executed the deed.[15]

To complicate things further, there is a third category of questionable deeds. If a deed is executed by a person "of unsound mind, but not entirely without understanding" who has not been judicially determined to be of unsound mind, the deed is not automatically void. It is, however, voidable by the

---

[14]Civil Code § 63. Minors living independently may also sometimes be considered emancipated (Civil Code § 61). We recommend, however, that unless someone under 18 meets the statutory requirements, the transfer be handled through a guardian.

[15]Civil Code §§ 38, 40.

grantor—that is, the grantor can change his mind later and bring a lawsuit to get the property back.[16] Most often, such actions are brought by a conservator who is later appointed to manage the person's affairs.

Example: Florence, an elderly woman, transfers her house to her nephew. A few months later, a court rules that she is incompetent, and a conservator is appointed for her. The conservator may sue the new owner on the ground that Florence was not of sound mind when she executed the deed. If the court finds for the conservator, it will rescind the deed, giving the property back to Florence.

If you think a deed may be challenged later based on the mental capacity of the person who signs it, see an attorney.

G. PERSONS WHO HAVE EXECUTED A POWER OF ATTORNEY

Giving someone the "power of attorney" gives him the power to take certain actions on your behalf. The person you appoint is called your "attorney in fact."

Power of attorney must be given in writing. When it gives someone authority to transfer or encumber real estate, it should also be recorded with the county recorder. If there is no written record that the person who signs the deed was in fact authorized to do so, the chain of title will have a gap in it.

Example: Sara signs a power of attorney that gives Ellen authority to act for her in all legal matters while she is in Europe for six months. This authorization includes signing a deed to the house Ellen and Sara co-own and are trying to sell. If they don't record the power of attorney with the county recorder in the county where the property is located, a subsequent title search would show that only Ellen signed the deed to the house. Without a record of the written authorization, the deed would appear ineffective to transfer Sara's interest in the property.

An attorney in fact must specify that he is acting for the owner of the property by signing the deed, for example, "Ellen Palmer, attorney in fact for Sara Puchinsky."

---

[16]Civil Code § 39.

Two kinds of powers of attorney are useful for property transfers:

• **A conventional power of attorney** gives the attorney in fact authority to act in specific matters or for a specific period of time, when someone knows he will be temporarily unable to take care of legal matters (for example, because he will be out of the country).

• **A durable power of attorney** is used when someone wants to ensure that if she should become incapacitated, a person she trusts will be empowered to make important decisions about medical attention and business affairs. Unlike a conventional power of attorney, it does not automatically end when the person becomes incapacitated. (A "springing" durable power of attorney takes effect only when the principal becomes incapacitated.)

For more information about powers of attorney, and tear-out power of attorney forms, see *The Power of Attorney Book* by Denis Clifford (Nolo Press).

C H A P T E R 4

HOW SHOULD THE NEW OWNERS TAKE TITLE?

After you've cleared up the question of who must sign the deed to transfer your property (Chapter 3), it's time to look at the other end of the transaction and decide how the recipients should take title to the property. You can't prepare a deed until you figure out how to specify the way title will be held by the new owners.

A. TRANSFERS TO ONE UNMARRIED RECIPIENT

If you're transferring property to one unmarried person, consider yourself lucky. You don't need to worry about choosing the form of the new owner's title; the recipient simply takes title in his name.

It's a good idea to point out on the deed itself that the recipient is unmarried, just so no one later has to wonder whether a spouse had a community property interest in the property transferred. Thus a deed to an unmarried woman would state, for example, that the current owner grants the property "to Elizabeth H. Bernstein, an unmarried woman."

Note: If you want to put property in trust for an unmarried person, see Section G below.

B. MORE THAN ONE UNMARRIED RECIPIENT

Unmarried persons to whom title is being transferred jointly may take title in one of three forms: a tenancy in common, joint tenancy, or partnership (in the partnership's name). This choice can have significant consequences when:

- the interest of a co-owner is later sold;
- the interests of all owners are sold at the same time; or
- a co-owner dies.

Unless the new owners are already in or want to form a partnership—two or more persons who own a business together—they will want to take title as joint tenants or tenants in common. We discussed the forms of ownership briefly in Chapter 3. We go into more detail here.[1] Partnerships are discussed in Section D below.

1. Shared Features of Joint Tenancy and Tenancy in Common

Tenancy in common and joint tenancy, the most common forms of co-ownership, share many features, including:

----

[1]Readers who have read the material in Chapter 3 on joint ownership will find some of the information repeated here. We apologize for the repetition, but it's virtually unavoidable because most readers probably didn't need to read the earlier version.

• **Equal right to use or sell the property.** No matter what shares joint owners have in real property,[2] no co-owner has the exclusive right to use or transfer a specific physical part of the property. Instead, each co-owner has, in legal jargon, an "undivided interest" in the property. Each may use the whole property and each is entitled to income from the whole property in proportion to his ownership share. For example, if three joint tenants (who always own equal shares) own a farm that is leased for $30,000 a year, each is entitled to $10,000.

In other words, if you own property as a joint tenant or tenant in common, you do not own a particular, physically defined half of the property. You may transfer only your particular share of the overall ownership.

Example: Joanne and Ed Fisher, brother and sister, each own a 1/2 interest in a 10-acre mountain lot they inherited from their parents. Informally, they agree that Ed will live on the south half of the property while Joanne will occupy the north half. Both Ed and Joanne build cabins on their portions. Later, Ed and Joanne have a feud and decide that 10 acres is too small for the two of them. Neither wishes to buy the other out. Joanne simply wants to sell her portion of the land and move to New York. Can she sell just five acres? No. Despite their arrangement, neither Ed nor Joanne owns a five-acre piece. Thus, Joanne can only sell her one-half interest in the ten acres as a whole (but see the discussion below on partitions).

Because co-owners are entitled to their proportionate share of income from the property, if Ed rented out his cabin three months a year for $200 a month, Joanne would be entitled to $300 (half of $600). If Ed owned a 90% interest in the property,[3] his share of the income would be $540 (90% of $600). As co-owners, Ed and Joanne are also responsible for their proportionate shares of expenses, including taxes, repairs and maintenance, and insurance. If Joanne pays more than her share of these costs, she is entitled to reimbursement from Ed. Similarly, if she damages the property, she must reimburse Ed for the reduction in market value of his interest.

• **Right to partition.** If one co-owner is unable to sell just his separate interest (as is often the case) and the co-owners can't agree on selling or dividing the property, any of them may request a partition from a court in the county where the land is located. Every tenant has an absolute right to obtain a partition of the property. No particular reason is necessary. The court usually orders that the property be sold and the proceeds divided among the co-tenants according to their ownership interests. The court can, however, order that the property be physically divided. How to file a partition action is beyond the scope of this book; a lawyer's advice will be needed.

---

[2]In joint tenancy, joint owners' shares must be equal; when property is held in a tenancy in common, shares can be unequal.

[3]Again, such an unequal division of shares would be possible only if the property were held in tenancy in common, not joint tenancy. See Section B.3 below.

CHANGING THE TERMS OF CO-OWNERSHIP BY CONTRACT

If co-owners are unhappy with the terms of the co-ownership—if, for example, they don't want to own "undivided interests" in the property, they can partition the property, either by simply executing new deeds or going to court. For example, Ed and Joanne could execute two deeds, each giving one of them five acres of the property.[4]

In some special situations, however, co-owners may not want simply to divide the property. Instead, they may want to make a separate agreement among themselves about the use of the property. For example, in some cities, restrictions on converting rental property to condominiums (that is, separate ownership of each unit) make it impossible for co-owners to divide ownership of a duplex or four-plex. The co-owners could, however, make a contract that gives each owner specific rights to use a certain part of the jointly-owned property.

Such contracts can be quite complicated, and local zoning ordinances and state laws may restrict their content. Before you make one, see a real estate attorney.

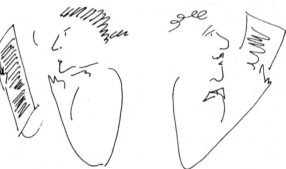

Now that we have explored how joint tenancy and tenancy in common, are alike, let's discuss each separately.

2. When to Use Tenancy in Common

Tenancy in common is the appropriate form of ownership for most co-owners unless they already have a close family relationship (in that case joint tenancy

---

[4]This would, however, necessitate having a surveyor draw up new legal descriptions of the property for the two deeds. Division of property is often also limited by local zoning laws.

—discussed below—may be more appropriate). Generally speaking, it is necessary to create a tenancy in common when:

• the new co-owners want to leave their interests in the property to someone other than their fellow co-owner(s); or

• the new co-owners want to own the property in unequal shares (e.g., one co-owner owns a two-thirds interest and another owns one-third).[5]

A big drawback to owning real property in tenancy in common has always been the necessity for probate when a co-owner dies. Probate can be avoided if the property is in a living trust or held in joint tenancy.

In California, any transfer of real property to two or more persons automatically creates a tenancy in common unless the deed says otherwise. No special words are necessary. This deed language would create a tenancy in common:

"to Darrell Buckner, Len Ryan, and Roberta Fernandez, as tenants in common."

So would this:

"to Nolan Gooden and Dwight Wilson."

3. When to Use Joint Tenancy

Joint tenancy, although useful in many situations, reduces the flexibility that a joint owner has in respect to his property interest. It is generally advisable for persons who:

• want the property to automatically (without probate) go to the surviving co-owners upon a co-owner's death; and

• want each joint owner to own an equal share of the property.

Probably the most significant feature of joint tenancy is that when one joint tenant dies, his interest in the property goes to the surviving joint tenants, even if his will contains a provision to the contrary. Probate proceedings are not necessary to effect the transfer, which can therefore be accomplished quickly and easily. For this reason, joint tenancy is often used by persons in a close, long-term personal relationship. It also used to be the preferred way for married couples to hold property. These days, (as discussed in Section C, below), married people in California usually hold their property as community property, a form of joint ownership that has some of the same consequences as joint tenancy and is often more advantageous from a tax standpoint.

Joint tenancy is not always the best way to avoid probate. Take the common situation of an older person who wants to keep control of property during her

---

[5]Remember that, regardless of the percentages of ownership, the ownership is in the whole property rather than a particular part of it.

lifetime, have it go to a child or other younger relative at her death, and avoid probate. She can accomplish most of these goals by putting the property in joint tenancy with the younger relative. The drawback to doing this is that she can't change her mind and take the property back once someone else's name is on the title. If, like King Lear, she is later confronted by an ungrateful child, thinks better of her generosity and wants the land back, she will find that she can't take back the gift.[6] If, on the other hand, she put the property in a living trust (which would also avoid probate; see Section F, below), naming her relative as beneficiary, she could at any time change the terms of the trust or terminate it altogether. If she didn't terminate the trust, when she died, the relative would inherit the entire property free of probate.

Joint tenants must own equal shares; you cannot create a joint tenancy in which one person owns, for example, a two-thirds interest in the property.

To create a joint tenancy, a deed must specify that the cotenants hold title as joint tenants or "with right of survivorship." The deed need not be titled "Joint Tenancy Deed" (though some are) as long as it designates the new owners as joint tenants.

Example: Here is what a deed from Joanne and Ed (from our earlier example) would look like if they wanted to become joint tenants:

JOINT TENANCY

---

[6]As Lear put it, "How sharper than a serpent's tooth it is to have a thankless child!" He obviously didn't know about revocable living trusts, which could have saved him a lot of trouble.

Recording requested by
    Joanne Hayden
    Edward Hayden
    3645 Eagle Creek Road
    Palmdale, CA 97329
and when recorded mail
this deed and tax statements to:

    same as above

For recorder's use

GRANT DEED

☒ This transfer is exempt from the documentary transfer tax.
☐ The documentary transfer tax is $_____ and is computed on
    ☐ the full value of the interest or property conveyed.
    ☐ the full value less the value of liens or encumbrances remaining thereon at the time of sale.
The property is located in ☒ an unincorporated area. ☐ the city of _____.

For a valuable consideration, receipt of which is hereby acknowledged,
    JOANNE HAYDEN and EDWARD HAYDEN, tenants in common,

hereby grant(s) to

    JOANNE HAYDEN and EDWARD HAYDEN, as joint tenants,

the following real property in the City of xxxxxxxxxxxxxxxxx County of ____Kern____,
California:

Tax Note: Although joint tenancy can be used to avoid probate, it will not avoid federal estate (inheritance) taxes. All property in which a decedent had any interest, including joint tenancy property that passes outside probate, is counted for federal estate tax purposes.[7]

---

[7]See Chapter 2, Section C. Joint tenancy and estate taxes are discussed in more detail in Clifford, *Plan Your Estate: Wills, Probate Avoidance, Trusts & Taxes* and Nissley, *How To Settle A Simple Estate* (Nolo Press).

FORMS OF REAL PROPERTY CO-OWNERSHIP

	Tenancy In Common	Joint Tenancy	Partnership
Creation	Deed must transfer property to 2 or more persons "as tenants in common" or without specifying how title is to be held.	Deed must say to X, Y and Z "as joint tenants" or "with right of survivorship."	Deed must say the to name of the partnership, or partnership funds must be used to buy it.
Shares of co-tenants	May be unequal (this is specified on the deed).	All joint tenants must own equal shares.	Determined by partnership agreement or Uniform Partnership Act.
Survivorship	On co-tenant's death, interest passes to heirs under intestate succession or beneficiaries under will or living trust.	Interest goes to surviving joint tenants even if will is to the contrary.	Interests usually go to partner's heirs or beneficiaries, but partnership agreement may limit this.
Probate	Interest left by will is subject to probate (simplified transfer procedures are available for community property left to spouse).	No probate necessary to transfer title to surviving joint tenants.	Interest left by will is subject to probate.
Termination	Co-tenants may jointly create joint tenancy by signing new deed. One may transfer his interest or get partition order from court.	Joint tenant may end joint tenancy (but keep his interest in the property) by transferring his interest to himself or another as tenants in common, or may obtain partition order from court.	Governed by partnership agreement or UPA.

Note: If you are not sure, after reading this section, how the new owners should take title, we recommend a consultation with a knowledgeable real estate professional or attorney. See Chapter 8 for a discussion of how to find and work with one.

C. TRANSFERS TO MARRIED RECIPIENTS

Married persons have several choices of how to take title to real property. Like unmarried co-owners, married couples may take title as joint tenants or tenants in common (see Section B above). Absent a strong reason to the contrary, however, we recommend that married couples take title to real estate as community property—that is, that they specify on the deed that the property is being held "as community property."

Note: A married person who wants to own real property separately, as an individual, can take title in her name alone and execute a separate written agreement with her spouse declaring the property to be separate, not community, property. See section 5 below.

1. Advantages of Community Property Ownership

This form of ownership allows survivors to avoid formal probate and offers a tax planning advantage as well. Let's consider each of these features in more detail.

a. Probate Avoidance

Property held in community property form goes directly to a surviving spouse without having to pass through probate, unless a will leaves it to someone else.

The surviving spouse need only file a simple petition (on a standard, pre-printed form used statewide) with the probate court.[8] This avoids not only lengthy delays in transferring title into the name of the survivor, but also probate fees.

WHAT IF YOU DON'T WANT TO LEAVE PROPERTY TO YOUR SPOUSE?

A spouse can leave community property, through a will, to someone other than the surviving spouse. If the will does not name someone to receive it, the deceased person's share of the community property goes to the surviving spouse.

If a married couple holds real property in joint tenancy when one of the spouses dies, the property goes to the surviving spouse, no matter what the deceased spouse's will says. As a practical matter, however, holding property in joint tenancy offers a spouse little assurance that he'll actually get the property when his spouse dies. It is a simple matter for a joint tenant, acting entirely on her own, to change the joint tenancy to a tenancy in common (which can be left by will) and then leave her interest in the property to someone else.

---

b. Tax Planning

Holding title as community property often makes it more convenient for a surviving spouse who inherits the property to qualify for special federal income tax treatment than does holding title in tenancy in common or joint tenancy.[9] It still may be possible to qualify for this treatment when the

---

[8]The community property petition and instructions for filling it out and filing it with the court are included in Julia Nissley's *How to Probate an Estate* (Nolo Press).

[9]We're talking about income tax here, not the gift and estate tax. Remember, property inherited by a surviving spouse is not subject to the gift/estate tax (Chapter 2, Section C).

property is not designated as community property on the deed, but it's more difficult. See section 4 below.

If you don't want to take our word for it that community property is a good idea, here's how the tax advantage for community property works. First, you need to know a little about how federal income tax is computed when a home is sold. Essentially, the difference between the sale price of the house and the price paid by the owners when they bought it (plus the cost of capital improvements) is taxable profit.[10]

Example: Carmen and Al buy a house in 1971 for $60,000. Over the years they make $10,000 in capital improvements,[11] and sell the place in 1987 for $150,000 (after costs of sale are subtracted). They must pay income tax on the $80,000 difference.

In tax lingo, the amount that Carmen and Al paid for the house, plus the cost of improvements, is their "tax basis" in the property (i.e., $70,000). From this basis, profit is figured. The increase in the house's value over the basis, as reflected in the selling price, is taxable income. Thus the higher the basis, the better, because less of the money received from selling the property is considered taxable profit. Here's how the numbers in our example look:

Sale of Carmen and Al's house:

$150,000 - $70,000	=	$80,000
Sale Price - Basis	=	Taxable Profit

When a property owner dies, the tax rules change. Specifically, the tax basis in the share of the property interest owned by the deceased person is automatically increased to the property's value at his death. The new owner's basis is referred to as a "stepped-up" basis.

Let's go back to Carmen and Al and assume that they owned their house as joint tenants or tenants in common (not community property) and that Carmen died and left her half-interest in the property to Al. At Carmen's death, the basis for her half of the property would increase from $35,000 (half of the $60,000 purchase price and $10,000 in improvements) to $75,000 (half of the value of the property at the time of her death). The basis in the other half of the property ($35,000) would remain the same. Al's total tax basis in the house would now be $110,000 ($75,000 plus $35,000). Now, when he sells the house for $150,000, he will have to pay income tax on the $40,000 difference between the

---

[10]Unless the money is reinvested in another house within 24 months, in which case taxation of some or all of the gain is deferred.

[11]Capital improvements are permanent improvements that increase the value of your property and have a useful life of more than a year—for example, new insulation or a new patio. Ordinary repairs and maintenance don't qualify as capital improvements.

new tax basis (created by Carmen's death) and the sales price. Here's how the numbers look:

Sale after Carmen's death, if house had been held as separate (not community) property:

$150,000 - $110,000   = $40,000
Sale Price - Basis   =   Taxable Profit

As you can see, a stepped-up basis reduces the amount of taxable income from the sale of property. Of course, a stepped-up tax basis isn't worth dying for, but it certainly eases the way for a surviving joint property owner. For example, if the survivor wants to sell a house with a stepped-up basis soon after the first spouse dies, he will owe tax only on any increase in value since the first spouse's death.

Now, finally, is when the advantage of having the property treated as community property comes in. For community property inherited by a surviving spouse, there is a bonus: all the community property, not just the one-half inherited by the surviving spouse (who already owned one-half, remember), qualifies for a "stepped-up" federal tax basis. Thus if Al and Carmen had held their house as community property, both Al's and Carmen's shares (not just Carmen's) would receive a stepped-up basis when Carmen died. The new basis, at Carmen's death, would be $150,000—the value of the entire property at the time she died. If Al sold the property for $150,000 after Carmen's death, he would owe no federal income tax on the transaction. The bottom line: the special stepped-up basis rule for community property makes it worthwhile for a married couple to hold their real estate "as community property."

Sale after Carmen's death, if house had been held as community property:

$150,000 - $150,000   = $0
Sale Price - Basis   =   Taxable Profit

2. Placing Property in Community Property Form

It is easy to place property in community property form when the deed is drawn up from scratch. Simply write the deed, for example, "to Carmen Rivera and Albert Rivera, as community property," or "to Carmen Rivera and Albert Rivera, as husband and wife."

Note: In the absence of a written agreement to the contrary, California law presumes jointly owned property to be community property under certain circumstances—if, for example, a couple divorces.[12] Rather than rely on this presumption, however, married couples should explicitly convert their jointly owned property to community property form to remove any uncertainty about what they intend.

If you want to change your current property ownership arrangement to community property, there are two ways to go about the task.

a. Sign a New Deed

The best way to change an existing joint ownership arrangement to community property is simply to execute a new deed to yourselves and record it in the county recorder's office.

Example: Carmen and Al, who purchased their home as joint tenants, execute and record a deed "from Carmen Rivera and Albert Rivera, as joint tenants, to Carmen Rivera and Albert Rivera, as community property."

b. Make a Community Property Agreement

Spouses can also recast jointly owned real estate as community property by signing an agreement to that effect and recording the agreement at the county recorder's office. The agreement must be in writing and must be recorded, just like a deed. Absent a special situation and a lawyer's advice, however, there is no good reason to write an agreement instead of a deed. A deed is simpler and is more readily understood and accepted by courts and government agencies.

Note: If a spouse contributes her separate property to a community property asset (e.g., makes mortgage payments from separate property on a community property home) and the couple divorces, the contributing spouse is entitled to reimbursement, unless there is a written agreement to the contrary.[13]

3. Placing Property in Joint Tenancy

Although holding title as community property is usually preferable, in certain situations, a married couple may prefer to put real estate in joint tenancy. For example, a bank or savings and loan may insist, for purposes of its own, that the property be held in joint tenancy.

Before you take the property as joint tenants, you should read Section B above, which discusses the features of joint tenancy. If you want to convert

---

[12]Civil Code § 4800.2.

[13]Civil Code § 4800.2. *California Marriage and Divorce Law,* by Warner, Ihara and Elias (Nolo Press) covers these subjects in much greater detail.

property you own as community property to joint tenancy form, you should execute a new deed from yourselves "as husband and wife" to yourselves "as joint tenants."

Divorce Note: Remember that even though the deed sets up a joint tenancy, California law will presume the property to be community property if you and your spouse divorce. If you want to defeat this presumption, you can either:

• State, on the deed, that the property is intended to be separate property of the spouses, not community property; or

• Sign a separate agreement (like the one in Section 4 below),

Here is how the deed would look:

Recording requested by
Diane and James Holst
290 Gabriel Way
Albany, CA 94706

and when recorded mail
this deed and tax statements to:

same as above

For recorder's use

GRANT DEED

☒ This transfer is exempt from the documentary transfer tax.
☐ The documentary transfer tax is $_____ and is computed on
    ☐ the full value of the interest or property conveyed.
    ☐ the full value less the value of liens or encumbrances remaining thereon at the time of sale.
The property is located in ☐ an unincorporated area. ☒ the city of __Albany_____ .

For a valuable consideration, receipt of which is hereby acknowledged,

      DIANE HOLST and JAMES HOLST, as husband and wife,

hereby grant(s) to

      DIANE HOLST and JAMES HOLST, in joint tenancy, to be held
      as separate, not community property,
the following real property in the City of __Albany_____ , County of __Alameda_____ ,
California:

4. Taking Property as Tenants in Common

Married couples rarely hold property as tenants in common. They might want to take title this way, however, if they decide that each will own separate (that is, not community) interests in the property.

Like joint tenancy property, however, property held in tenancy in common is presumed to be community property, absent a written agreement to the contrary, when it comes to dividing up a couple's property at divorce. Thus if you don't want the property divided like community property (a 50-50 split unless one spouse can show that he contributed more to its purchase or improvement), you must include a statement to that effect on the deed (see section 3 above) or make a separate written agreement setting out your wishes. Here is a sample agreement:

MARITAL PROPERTY AGREEMENT

Diane Holst and James Kelvin, husband and wife, agree as follows:

1. We purchased the apartment building at 9347 24th Street, Anaheim, California, with community property funds and Diane's separate property.
2. We hold title to the building as tenants in common.
3. Because of Diane's greater investment in the building and her efforts in managing it, she shall be entitled to 80% of the value of the building, and James shall be entitled to 20%, if our marriage ends in dissolution.
4. We intend this document to rebut the presumption of current Civil Code § 4800.2 that property held in joint title is community property. We do not wish the property to be treated as community property for purposes of property division at dissolution.

Dated: _____   _____(signature)_____

_____   _____

State of California
County of _____ } ss.

On _____, _____, known to me or proved by satisfactory evidence to be the person(s) whose name(s) is/are subscribed above, personally appeared before me, a Notary Public for California, and acknowledged that _____ executed this deed.

_____   [SEAL]
Signature of Notary

---

5. Taking Title as Separate Property of One Spouse

If title is to be put in the name of one married individual, it's best to execute and record an agreement declaring the couple's intent that the property be held as one spouse's separate property. Otherwise, if they divorce and disagree about ownership of the property, a court will characterize the property as community or separate according to what kind of funds (community or separate) paid for it, not whose name appears on the deed. Because it isn't always clear what type of property was used to pay for improvements, taxes, etc., the fight can be nasty.

Here is a sample agreement to get your understanding in writing:

COMMUNITY PROPERTY AGREEMENT

We, Brian Morgan and Laura Stein, husband and wife, hereby agree that:

1. Brian Morgan holds title to a vacation cabin at Lake Tahoe.

2. Although the cabin was purchased with savings that were community property, we intend it to be the separate property of Brian Morgan.

3. We make this agreement in light of the fact that Brian contributed more to purchase of the cabin than did Laura and that upon Brian's death, we both want the cabin to be inherited by Scott Morgan, Brian's son.

Dated: _____   _____(signature)_____

_____   _____

State of California
County of _____} ss.

On _____, _____, known to me or proved by satisfactory evidence to be the person(s) whose name(s) is/are subscribed above, personally appeared before me, a Notary Public for California, and acknowledged that _____ executed this deed.

_____   [SEAL]
Signature of Notary

D. TRANSFERS TO PARTNERSHIPS

Partnerships are often formed when people decide to buy real estate together. To transfer real property to a partnership, the deed should be made out to the name the partnership does business under (the fictitious business name on file with the county or state), or to the partners by name.

"to Elm Street Books, a partnership" or

"to Linda Stone and Blake Herbert, a partnership."

What the partners can do with the property once it is transferred to the partnership is governed either by the partnership agreement or, in the absence of an agreement, the Uniform Partnership Act.[14]

Note: Property acquired with partnership funds is presumed to belong to the partnership, absent an agreement to the contrary.

E. TRANSFERS TO CORPORATIONS

A corporation takes property in the corporation's name. You must specify the entity clearly so that there will be no confusion over who actually owns the property. Only a legal entity—a person, a corporation, or a partnership—can own property. If you don't name one of them to receive it, the transfer could be invalidated.

Example: Jody wants to put property in the name of the flower shop she operates with her husband. The shop's name is "Jody and Don's Flower Shop" However, it was officially incorporated as "Jo-Don Flowers, Inc." The deed

---

[14]Calif. Corporations Code § 15001 et seq. See *The Partnership Book,* by Clifford and Warner (Nolo Press).

should be made out "to Jo-Don Flowers, Inc.," not to "Jody and Don's Flower Shop."

F. TRANSFERS TO MINORS

There is very seldom a good reason for giving real estate directly to a minor (someone less than 18 years old). In most cases, an adult will have to manage the property anyway, which means you must set up a trust or property custodianship.[15] We discuss these options below.

1. To a Custodian Under the Uniform Transfers to Minors Act

The best way to give property to a minor is to transfer it to an adult as a "custodian" for the minor, under the California Uniform Transfers To Minors Act.[16] This can be done either in a deed or in a will; most often, a will is used because there is rarely a good reason to want to transfer real property to a minor while the owner is still alive and able to manage it himself.[17]

A property custodian is similar to a trustee (see Section G below), but her rights and duties are outlined by statute instead of by you. A custodian must be prudent in her management of the property and must keep certain records.

Under the Act, you may appoint only one person to manage property for a minor, but you can nominate alternate custodians to take over in case your first choice is unable or unwilling to serve. You must separately designate a custodian for each minor to whom you're giving property. A deed creating a custodianship would look like this:

---

[15]If you want to leave real property to a minor through your will, you will probably want to set it up so that when you die the minor gets it in trust if he is not yet of age. A trust set up in a will is called a testamentary trust (one established by a living person is called a living or inter vivos trust).

[16]Probate Code §§ 3900 et seq.

[17]Estate tax considerations may prompt some people to give away property before they die, but most people don't need to worry because their estates will not exceed the $600,0000 amount that is exempt from the tax. See Chapter 2, Section C.

Recording requested by

Grace Henry
342 Grove Street
Mendocino, CA 93702

and when recorded mail
this deed and tax statements to:

same as above

For recorder's use

GRANT DEED

☒ This transfer is exempt from the documentary transfer tax.
☐ The documentary transfer tax is $_____ and is computed on
   ☐ the full value of the interest or property conveyed.
   ☐ the full value less the value of liens or encumbrances remaining thereon at the time of sale.
The property is located in ☐ an unincorporated area. ☒ the city of <u>Mendocino</u> .

For a valuable consideration, receipt of which is hereby acknowledged,

    Sarah J. Hooper

hereby grant(s) to

    Grace Henry, as custodian for David Campbell until age 21,
    under the California Uniform Transfers to Minors Act.

the following real property in the City of <u>Mendocino</u> , County of <u>Mendocino</u> ,
California:

The transfer becomes effective when the deed is recorded. It is irrevocable (you can't take it back). The custodian transfers the property to the minor outright when the minor turns 18, unless the donor has specified another age (up to 25) at which he is to receive the property (see sample deed above). This offers more flexibility than simply transferring the property to the minor; in that case, the minor gets full control of the property when he turns 18.

2. To the Minor Directly

A minor can take title to real estate, although he can't sell or mortgage it.[18] If the minor has a parent or guardian, that person will take care of any property given the minor, even though the transfer should be made directly to the minor by naming him in a deed like this: "to Scott Hawthorne, a minor."

G. TRANSFERS TO LIVING TRUSTS

A revocable living (inter vivos) trust is a probate avoidance device established by a living person, not in a will.[19] The owner of property (the trustor) transfers it to the trust and names a trustee (to manage the property) and a beneficiary. The terms of the trust usually instruct the trustee to transfer outright ownership of the property to the beneficiary when the trustor dies. If the same property were left by will, it would probably have to go through probate, which takes months and can be costly.

Commonly, when someone sets up this kind of trust he names himself as trustee. This allows him to keep control over his property while he is alive and make sure it goes to the beneficiary, without probate, when he dies. If he changes his mind at any time, he can simply revoke the trust or change the beneficiary.

If the owner of the property is the trustee, the trust document usually names a successor trustee to take over when he dies. The successor trustee is directed to give the property to the beneficiary.

The trustee takes title not in just her own name but as, for example, "Sandra Connelly, trustee . . . ." In most cases, because the trustee is none other than yourself, you simply transfer the property from yourself to yourself as trustee. Obviously, revoking the trust is a simple matter when you are the trustee; you merely transfer the property back to yourself.

To create a trust for real property, you must sign a trust document that appoints a trustee and sets out the terms of the trust (how the trustee is to manage the property, whether or not the trust is revocable, when ownership should be transferred to the beneficiary, etc.).

Because this book is about deeds rather than estate planning, we don't discuss trusts in general or tell you how to set them up. Rather, we assume that you have established the trust, or plan to do so, with the help of a lawyer or a

---

[18]There is one exception: an "emancipated minor" has all the rights of an adult. See Chapter 3, Section F.

[19]Living trusts can also be irrevocable; it's up to the person who sets up the trust. Whether or not the trust can be revoked is specified in the trust document that creates the trust.

self-help guide such as Denis Clifford's *Plan Your Estate: Wills, Probate Avoidance, Trusts & Taxes* (Nolo Press).

Here, we help you with two aspects of creating or terminating a trust for real property, both of which require execution of a deed:

• transferring property into the trust once it is established, and

• transferring the property out of the trust when the time comes for the property to be distributed (see Chapter 3, Section C).

A trust is not effective unless you actually transfer the property, via a standard deed, to the trust. This is accomplished by making the transfer to the trustee. To transfer the property, you must fill out and sign a deed naming the trustee, like this:

Recording requested by

Marjorie Simmons
499 Sycamore Street
Anaheim, CA 98732

and when recorded mail
this deed and tax statements to:

same as above

For recorder's use

GRANT DEED

☒ This transfer is exempt from the documentary transfer tax.
☐ The documentary transfer tax is $_____ and is computed on
   ☐ the full value of the interest or property conveyed.
   ☐ the full value less the value of liens or encumbrances remaining thereon at the time of sale.
The property is located in ☐ an unincorporated area. ☒ the city of ____Anaheim____.

For a valuable consideration, receipt of which is hereby acknowledged,

    MARJORIE SIMMONS

hereby grant(s) to

    MARJORIE SIMMONS, in trust for David R. Maclean,

the following real property in the City of ____Anaheim____, County of ____Orange____, California:

The deed should be recorded with the county recorder in the county where the real property is located (see Chapter 7).

Note for married trustors: As with any transfer from a married person, both you and your spouse should sign the deed transferring real property to a trust. Even if you are sure that the property you are putting in trust is your separate property, we recommend being on the safe side and having your spouse sign. We explain why in Chapter 3, Section A.

What's next: Once you have decided how the new owners of the property should take title, you're ready to go to Chapter 6 and prepare your deed.

C H A P T E R   5

DEEDS OF TRUST

As discussed in Chapter 4, a trust deed is not a conventional deed used to transfer ownership to real property; it is really the functional equivalent of a mortgage.[1] Like a mortgage, a trust deed makes a piece of real property security for a loan to the property owner. If the loan is not repaid on time, the property can be sold (foreclosed on) by the lender and the proceeds used to pay it off. This chapter explains how trust deeds are used and how to fill one out.

---

[1]In California, deeds of trust have virtually replaced mortgages because they allow a less cumbersome process if the borrower defaults. Deeds of trust came into favor because traditional mortgages required a lawsuit for foreclosure; the lender ("mortgagee") did not have a power of sale. Now, however, mortgages commonly have power of sale. Under either a mortgage or deed of trust, detailed statutes govern foreclosure. See Civil Code §§ 2920-2944. Foreclosure on a trust deed takes at least four months and requires scrupulous attention to the statutory requirements. For example, a defaulting borrower must be given a warning that is worded a certain way and is printed in a certain size of type. Civil Code § 2924c. For that reason, foreclosures are almost always handled by specialized companies that do little else. We don't discuss all the complicated rules about foreclosing on deeds of trust—that would take another small book.

A. HOW TRUST DEEDS WORK

A trust deed is used in tandem with a promissory note that sets out the amount and terms of the loan. The borrower signs the note, which is a written promise to repay the borrowed money. A trust deed, which makes the property security for the loan, is also prepared. If the borrower defaults on the note, the trust deed allows the property to be sold (by the person named in the trust deed as the trustee) and the lender repaid from the proceeds. Whatever money is left, after the lender is paid and the costs of sale paid for, goes to the borrower.

The trustee's power of sale. When the property owner executes a trust deed, he gives a third party, the "trustee," legal ownership of the property. The trustee is usually a title company or real estate broker. The trustee has no control over the property as long as the borrower makes the agreed-upon payments on the loan and fulfills the promises in the trust deed (e.g., to take care of the property and keep up insurance). If he defaults, however, the trustee has the power to sell the property, without having to file a court action, to pay off the loan.

DEEDS OF TRUST: CAST OF CHARACTERS

Trustor: The trustor is the borrower; he owns the property but signs the trust deed making giving the trustee power to sell it if he defaults on the loan.

Trustee: The trustee named in a trust deed does not exercise any control over the property; he has only the power to sell the property if the loan the trust deed secures is defaulted on. Frequently, a title insurance company serves as trustee.

Beneficiary: The lender is the beneficiary; if the property is sold, the lender is repaid from the proceeds.

Example: Jan wants to borrow money from her brother Loren, using her house as security for the loan. He doesn't doubt that she'll pay him, but if for some reason she can't (because she dies, becomes incapacitated, or goes bankrupt), he wants to be assured of getting the property back without having to file a lawsuit. She signs a promissory note for the amount of the loan and a deed of trust that gives a trustee power to sell the house if she defaults on the loan. She is the trustor; Loren, who loaned her the money, is the beneficiary of the trust deed. As trustee, the trust deed names the ABC Title Company (how to pick a trustee is discussed in Section C below). The trustee has no powers unless Jan defaults on the loan and Loren wants to foreclose on the loan.

Reconveyance of title: When the loan is paid off, the trustee's and lender's interests end. The trustee executes and records a deed that reconveys title to the property back to the owner (the person who borrowed the money).[2]

Multiple deeds of trust. When a property owner borrows money from a family member, there is often already a deed of trust on the property—the one signed when an institutional lender financed the purchase of the property. That's no problem—an owner can keep signing trust deeds as long as lenders are willing to lend money on the property. A lender won't be willing to accept a trust deed as security for a loan when it appears that, if the property is foreclosed on and sold, the proceeds of sale won't be enough to pay off its loan.

Example: Suzanne asks Adam for a loan of $25,000, offering her house as security. The house, which is worth $150,000, already has a $120,000 deed of trust on it. Adam says no. He knows that if the house were sold at a foreclosure sale it might well bring less than it's really worth, and that by the time the first trust deed holder and the costs of sale were paid off, he wouldn't get his money back.

Who gets paid if the property is sold and there's not enough money to pay off all the encumbrances on the property (deeds of trust and liens)? In general, liens are paid off in the order they were recorded. Thus the holder of a second trust deed (often just called a "second") only gets what's left after the first trust deed is paid off. State statutes, however, contain a fairly complicated system of preferences and priorities. Property tax liens, for example, must always be paid off first.

Example: Stephen defaults on a loan from Rebecca secured by a deed of trust on his property. He is also behind in his property tax payments, and the county has recorded a tax lien on the property. If Rebecca forecloses on the property and has the property sold, the tax lien will be paid first, and what's left over will be applied to the debt secured by the deed of trust.

Reminder: A trust deed is **not** used to transfer property to a living trust. The terminology is confusingly similar, but trust deeds and living trusts have almost nothing else in common. A living trust is a probate avoidance device; it is not used to provide security for a loan. Transfers to living trusts are discussed in Chapter 4, Section G.

---

[2]The trustee transfers title with a grant deed (sometimes called a "deed of reconveyance" on printed forms). Chapter 6 contains instructions for filling out a grant deed.

Recording requested by

Helen D. Whiteclyffe

and when recorded mail this deed and tax statements to:
Helen D. Whiteclyffe
72 Bloomsbury Road
Mount Hamilton, CA 93766

For recorder's use

DEED OF TRUST

James Chadwick _____, Trustor, hereby grants __XYZ Title Company_____, Trustee, with power of sale, the following real property in the City of __Mount Hamilton__, County of __Santa Clara__, California:

SEE LEGAL DESCRIPTION ATTACHED HERETO AND INCORPORATED HEREIN AS EXHIBIT A

together with its rents, issues and profits, subject to the Beneficiary's rights to collect and apply rents, issues and profits, given by paragraph 10 of the provisions incorporated herein by reference.

This deed is executed to secure payment of the debt evidenced by a promissory note signed by Trustor March 21 , 198 in favor of Helen D. Whiteclyffe _____, Beneficiary, in the sum of $44,500.00_____.

Trustor agrees that by execution and delivery of the deed of trust and the note it secures that provisions one through 14 of the fictitious deed of trust recorded October 18, 1961 in Santa Barbara and Sonoma Counties and in all other counties October 23, 1961, as set out below, are adopted and incorporated herein and that Trustor will observe those provisions.

The fictitious deed of trust incorporated herein is recorded with the county recorder of each California county as follows:

COUNTY	BOOK	PAGE	COUNTY	BOOK	PAGE	COUNTY	BOOK	PAGE	COUNTY	BOOK	PAGE
Alameda	435	684	Kings	792	833	Placer	895	301	Shasta	684	528
Alpine	1	250	Lake	362	39	Plumas	151	5	Sierra	29	335
Amador	104	348	Lassen	171	471	Riverside	3005	523	Siskiyou	468	181
Butte	1145	1	Los Angeles	T2055	899	Sacramento	4331	62	Solano	1105	182
Calaveras	145	152	Madera	810	170	San Benito	271	383	Sonoma	1851	689
Colusa	296	617	Marin	1508	339	San Bernardino	5567	61	Stanislaus	1715	1456
Contra Costa	3978	47	Mariposa	77	292	San Francisco	A332	905	Sutter	572	297
Del Norte	78	414	Mendocino	579	530	San Joaquin	2470	311	Tehama	491	289
El Dorado	568	456	Merced	1547	538	San Luis Obispo	1151	12	Trinity	93	366
Fresno	4626	572	Modoc	184	851	San Mateo	4078	420	Tulare	2294	275
Glenn	422	184	Mono	52	429	Santa Barbara	1878	860	Tuolumne	135	47
Humboldt	657	527	Monterey	2194	538	Santa Clara	5336	342	Ventura	2062	386
Imperial	1091	501	Napa	639	86	Santa Cruz	1431	494	Yolo	653	245
Inyo	147	598	Nevada	305	320	San Diego	Series 2	Page	Yuba	334	486
Kern	3427	60	Orange	5869	611		Book 1961	183887			

A copy of any Notice of Default and any Notice of Sale under this deed of trust shall be mailed to Trustor at:
James Chadwick, 88761 Primrose Place, Mount Hamilton, CA 93766

Date: March 27, 198 _____   _James Chadwick_____
                                Signature of Trustor

                                _____
                                Signature of Trustor

State of California
County of Santa Clara) ss.
On March 27 , 198__ James Chadwick_____, known to me or proved by satisfactory evidence to be the person(s) whose name(s) is/are subscribed above, personally appeared before me, a Notary Public for California, and acknowledged that _he_ executed this deed.

_Lisa Samuels_____   [SEAL]
Signature of Notary

B. HOW TO FILL OUT A TRUST DEED AND PROMISSORY NOTE

As explained above, a trust deed makes real estate security for a loan. Thus if you have a trust deed, you will also need to prepare a promissory note that provides written evidence of the underlying debt. We explain how to draw up both the deed and the note.

Basically, a trust deed must identify the parties to the transaction and the property being given as security. It also must contain a statement that the deed of trust secures the obligation to repay a certain amount to the beneficiary. And, like other deeds, the signed original should be notarized, recorded and delivered to the beneficiary. Because parts of a trust deed look a lot like a grant deed, these instructions occasionally refer you to Section B of Chapter 6, which contains instructions for filling out grant and quitclaim deeds.

1. The Deed of Trust

Here are instructions for filling out the deed of trust included in the appendix of this book. The letters correspond to the lettered blanks in the trust deed shown below.

Note: Trust deeds are exempt from the documentary transfer tax, so the deed form doesn't include tax information.[3]

---

[3]Rev. and Tax. Code § 11921.

a. Recording Information

The owner/borrower will want to receive the deed and property tax statements, so her name goes in this space. (Chapter 7 explains the recording system.)

b. Identification of the Trustor

The name of the trustor—the person borrowing the money and giving his property as security—goes in this blank. The names of all owners of the property, and their spouses, must be included to give the entire property (all owners' interests in the property) as security. A co-owner can only give as security his interest in the property. In other words, a lender wants to be sure that all owners and their spouses sign the deed of trust as a condition of lending the money (unless the lender is willing to take as security one co-owner's interest in property). The rules for who must sign a deed of trust are the same as for other deeds. See Chapter 3.

c. Identification of the Trustee

The second blank contains the name of the trustee. The trustee, remember, has no rights or responsibilities unless the borrower defaults on the underlying loan. If the borrower does default, the trustee has the power to sell the property to pay off the loan.

In the most common kind of real estate transactions, where a bank or savings and loan finances the purchase of real estate, the trustee is almost always a title or trust company. Sometimes real estate brokers act as trustees.

Attorneys commonly write in the name of a title company as trustee on a trust deed, without consulting the title company. Title companies even give out trust deed forms with their names already printed in the "trustee" space. They don't mind being named as trustee because a trustee has nothing to do unless the borrower defaults. If the borrower pays off the loan without defaulting (as happens in most cases), the title company then executes and records a deed reconveying the property to the borrower. The fee for that is about $75 to $100.

If foreclosure becomes necessary, most title or escrow companies[4] turn the deed over to a professional foreclosure firm, which will charge the lender approximately $1,000 up front to start the process. When the property is sold, the fee is paid from the proceeds.

---

[4]In northern California, title companies usually serve as escrow holders; in southern California, title and escrow companies are usually separate.

Recording requested by

(a)

and when recorded mail this deed and tax statements to:

For recorder's use

DEED OF TRUST

_____(b)_____, Trustor, hereby grants _____(c)_____, Trustee,
with power of sale, the following real property in the City of _____, County of _____,
California:

(d)

together with its rents, issues and profits, subject to the Beneficiary's rights to collect and apply rents, issues and profits,
given by paragraph 10 of the provisions incorporated herein by reference.

(e) This deed is executed to secure payment of the debt evidenced by a promissory note signed by Trustor _____, 19___
in favor of_____, Beneficiary, in the sum of $_____.

(f) Trustor agrees that by execution and delivery of the deed of trust and the note it secures that provisions one through 14 of
the fictitious deed of trust recorded October 18, 1961 in Santa Barbara and Sonoma Counties and in all other counties
October 23, 1961, as set out below, are adopted and incorporated herein and that Trustor will observe those provisions.

The fictitious deed of trust incorporated herein is recorded with the county recorder of each California county as follows:

COUNTY	BOOK	PAGE	COUNTY	BOOK	PAGE	COUNTY	BOOK	PAGE	COUNTY	BOOK	PAGE
Alameda	435	684	Kings	792	833	Placer	895	301	Shasta	684	528
Alpine	1	250	Lake	362	39	Plumas	151	5	Sierra	29	335
Amador	104	348	Lassen	171	471	Riverside	3005	523	Siskiyou	468	181
Butte	1145	1	Los Angeles	T2055	899	Sacramento	4331	62	Solano	1105	182
Calaveras	145	152	Madera	810	170	San Benito	271	383	Sonoma	1851	689
Colusa	296	617	Marin	1508	339	San Bernardino	5567	61	Stanislaus	1715	1456
Contra Costa	3978	47	Mariposa	77	292	San Francisco	A332	905	Sutter	572	297
Del Norte	78	414	Mendocino	579	530	San Joaquin	2470	311	Tehama	491	289
El Dorado	568	456	Merced	1547	538	San Luis Obispo	1151	12	Trinity	93	366
Fresno	4626	572	Modoc	184	851	San Mateo	4078	420	Tulare	2294	275
Glenn	422	184	Mono	52	429	Santa Barbara	1878	860	Tuolumne	135	47
Humboldt	657	527	Monterey	2194	538	Santa Clara	5336	342	Ventura	2062	386
Imperial	1091	501	Napa	639	86	Santa Cruz	1431	494	Yolo	653	245
Inyo	147	598	Nevada	305	320	San Diego	Series 2	Page	Yuba	334	486
Kern	3427	60	Orange	5889	611		Book 1961	183887			

A copy of any Notice of Default and any Notice of Sale under this deed of trust shall be mailed to Trustor at: (g)

_____

Date:_____ (h)   _____
                                Signature of Trustor

                                _____
                                Signature of Trustor

State of California
County of _____ } ss.

On _____19___ _____, known to me or proved by satisfactory evidence to
be the person(s) whose name(s) is/are subscribed above, personally appeared before me, a Notary Public for California,
and acknowledged that _____ executed this deed. (i)

                                                        [SEAL]

_____
Signature of Notary

d. Description of the Property

The trust deed must adequately describe the property that is being given as security. Usually you can just copy the description from the old deed, or attach a photocopy of the old description as "Exhibit A," and type in "see Exhibit A, attached" in the space allowed for the description. If for some reason you can't, or you don't trust that description, see Chapter 6, Section B, Item 7 for instructions.

e. Reference to the Promissory Note

This statement identifies the promissory note that was executed to evidence the underlying debt (a tear-out note is in the Appendix). You should fill in the date the note was signed, the amount of the debt, and the name of the person to whom the debt is owed. That person is the beneficiary of the trust deed, because if the property is sold to pay off the debt, the proceeds will go to repay her.

MODIFYING THE STANDARD DEED OF TRUST

If you wish, you can add clauses to the standard trust deed. We recommend, however, that you discuss your changes with a lawyer.
If you're the borrower, you may want to have one of these clauses in the deed:

• Option to pay off the note in full or part at a discount This rewards the borrower for paying off the note early.
• No due-on-sale clause. This eliminates the need to obtain the seller's approval of the purchaser if the borrower sells the property.
If you're selling the property and financing the sale, you may want to consider these options:
• Penalty for prepayment.
• Late charges for payments made more than ten days after the due date.
• Due-on-sale clause.
• Right to inspect the property and have the borrower provide loan application information. This helps the lender if she decides to sell the note to an investor.

---

f. Incorporation of the Fictitious Deed of Trust

In this paragraph, the trustor (the person giving his property as security) agrees to abide by a set of provisions contained in a standard "fictitious" deed of trust that has been recorded in every county in California. (Not recording the same piece of paper every time saves a few dollars in recording fees.) By incorporating the fictitious deed of trust, the borrower promises to keep the property in good repair, keep fire insurance up to date, pay property taxes on time, and otherwise protect the lender's investment. If the borrower breaks one of these promises, the trustee can foreclose on the property. The fictitious deed of trust also sets out the trustee's powers in case the borrower defaults on the loan.

The list of covenants in the fictitious deed of trust is printed on the back of the actual trust deed, but that page doesn't get recorded. The front page of the trust deed (which is recorded) simply refers to the fictitious deed of trust that has already been recorded in each county. The deed lists the location of the copy of the fictitious deed of trust in each county's official records.

g. Trustor's Address

Fill in the trustor's (borrower's) address here. This information is required by law.[5] It tells the trustee where to notify the property owner of any steps taken toward selling the property to pay off the debt.

h. Date and Signatures

Here, the trustors (borrowers) should sign and date the deed. All named trustors must sign.

i. Acknowledgment (Notarization)

A notary public fills in this section. See Item 12 of Chapter 6, Section B for instructions on how to get your deed notarized.

---

[5]Govt. Code § 27321.5.

DO NOT RECORD

The following is a copy of provisions (1) to (14), inclusive, of the fictitious deed of trust, recorded in each county in California, as stated in the foregoing Deed of Trust and incorporated by reference in said Deed of Trust as being a part thereof as if set forth at length therein.

To Protect the Security of This Deed of Trust, Trustor agrees:

(1) To keep said property in good condition and repair; not to remove or demolish any building thereon; to complete or restore promptly, and in good and workmanlike manner, any building which may be constructed, damaged or destroyed thereon and to pay when due all claims for labor performed and materials furnished therefore; to comply with all laws affecting said property or requiring any alterations or improvements to be made thereon; not to commit or permit waste thereof; not to commit, suffer or permit any act upon said property in violation of law; to cultivate, irrigate, fertilize, fumigate, prune and do all other acts which, from the character or use of said property, may be reasonably necessary, the specific enumerations herein not excluding the general.

(2) To provide, maintain and deliver to Beneficiary fire insurance satisfactory to and with loss payable to Beneficiary. The amount collected under any fire or other insurance policy may be applied by Beneficiary upon any indebtedness secured hereby and in such order as Beneficiary may determine, or at option of Beneficiary the entire amount so collected or any part thereof may be released to Trustor. Such application or release shall not cure or waive any default or notice of default hereunder or invalidate any act done pursuant to such notice.

(3) To appear in and defend any action or proceeding purporting to affect the security hereof or the rights or powers of Beneficiary or Trustee; and to pay all costs and expenses, including cost of evidence of title and attorney's fees in a reasonable sum, in any such action or proceeding in which Beneficiary or Trustee may appear, and in any suit brought by Beneficiary to foreclose this Deed.

(4) To pay: at least ten days before delinquency all taxes and assessments affecting said property, including assessments, on appurtenant water stock; when due, all incumbrances, charges and liens, with interest, on said property or any part thereof, which appear to be prior or superior hereto; all costs, fees and expenses of this Trust.

Should Trustor fail to make any payment or to do any act as herein provided, then Beneficiary or Trustee, but without obligation so to do and without notice to or demand upon Trustor and without releasing Trustor from any obligation hereof, may: make or do the same in such manner and to such extent as either may deem necessary to protect the security hereof, Beneficiary or Trustee being authorized to enter upon said property for such purposes; appear in and defend any action or proceeding purporting to affect the security hereof or the rights or powers of Beneficiary or Trustee; pay, purchase, contest or compromise any incumbrance, charge or lien which in the judgment of either appears to be prior or superior hereto; and, in exercising any such powers, pay necessary expenses, employ counsel and pay his reasonable fees.

(5) To pay immediately and without demand all sums so expended by Beneficiary or Trustee, with interest from date of expenditure at the amount allowed by law in effect at the date hereof, and to pay for any statement provided for by law in effect at the date hereof, regarding the obligation secured hereby any amount demanded by the Beneficiary not to exceed the maximum allowed by law at the time when said statement is demanded.

(6) That any award of damages in connection with any condemnation for public use of or injury to said property or any part thereof is hereby assigned and shall be paid to Beneficiary who may apply or release such moneys received by him in the same manner and with the same effect as above provided for disposition of proceeds of fire or other insurance.

(7) That by accepting payment of any sum secured hereby after its due date, Beneficiary does not waive his right either to require prompt payment when due of all other sums so secured or to declare default for failure so to pay.

(8) That at any time or from time to time, without liability therefor and without notice, upon written request of Beneficiary and presentation of this Deed and said note for endorsement, and without affecting the personal liability of any person for payment of the indebtedness secured hereby, Trustee may: reconvey any part of said property; consent to the making of any map or plat thereof; join in granting any easement thereon; or join in any extension agreement or any agreement subordinating the lien or charge hereof.

(9) That upon written request of Beneficiary stating that all sums secured hereby have been paid, and upon surrender of this Deed and said note to Trustee for cancellation and retention and upon payment of its fees, Trustee shall reconvey, without warranty, the property then held hereunder. The recitals in such reconveyance of any matters or facts shall be conclusive proof of the truthfulness thereon. The grantee in such reconveyance may be described as "the person or persons legally entitled thereto." Five years after issuance of such full reconveyance, Trustee may destroy said note and this Deed (unless directed in such request to retain them).

(10) That as additional security, Trustor hereby gives to and confers upon Beneficiary the right, power and authority, during the continuance of these Trusts, to collect the rents, issues and profits of said property, reserving unto Trustor the right, prior to any default by Trustor in payment of any indebtedness secured hereby or in performance of any agreement hereunder, to collect and retain such rents, issues and profits as they become due and payable. Upon any such default, Beneficiary may at any time without notice, either in person, by agent or by a receiver to be appointed by a court, and without regard to the adequacy of any security for the indebtedness hereby secured, enter upon and take possession of said property or any part thereof, in his own name sue for or otherwise collect such rents, issues and profits, including those past due and unpaid, and apply the same, less costs and expenses of operation and collection, including reasonable attorney's fees, upon any indebtedness secured hereby, and in such order as Beneficiary may determine. The entering upon and taking possession of said property, the collection of such rents, issues and profits, and the application thereof as aforesaid, shall not cure or waive any default or notice of default hereunder or invalidate any act done pursuant to such notice.

(11) That upon default by Trustor in payment of any indebtedness secured hereby or in performance of any agreement hereunder, Beneficiary may declare all sums secured hereby immediately due and payable by delivery to Trustee of written declaration of default and demand for sale and of written notice of default and of election to cause to be sold said property, which notice Trustee shall cause to be filed for record. Beneficiary also shall deposit with Trustee this Deed, said note and all documents evidencing expenditures secured hereby.

After the lapse of such time as may then be required by law following the recordation of said notice of default, and notice of sale having been given as then required by law, Trustee, without demand on Trustor, shall sell said property at the time and place fixed by it in said notice of sale, either as a whole or in separate parcels, and in such order as it may determine, at public auction to the highest bidder for cash in lawful money of the United States, payable at time of sale. Trustee may postpone sale of all or any portion of said property by public announcement at such time and place of sale, and from time to time thereafter may postpone such sale by public announcement at the time fixed by the preceeding postponement. Trustee shall deliver to such purchaser its deed conveying the property so sold, but without any covenant or warranty, express or implied. The recitals in such deed of any matters or facts shall be conclusive proof of the truthfulness thereof. Any person, including Trustor, Trustee, or Beneficiary as hereinafter defined, may purchase at such sale.

After deducting all costs, fees and expenses of Trustee and of this Trust, including cost of evidence of title in connection with sale, Trustee shall apply the proceeds of sale to payment of: all sums expended under the terms hereof, not then repaid, with accrued interest at the amount allowed by law in effect at the date hereof; all other sums then secured hereby; and the remainder, if any, to the person or persons legally entitled thereto.

(12) Beneficiary, or any successor in ownership of any indebtedness secured hereby, may from time to time, by instrument in writing, substitute a successor or successors to any Trustee named herein or acting hereunder which instrument, executed by the Beneficiary and duly acknowledged and recorded in the office of the recorder of the county or counties where said property is situated, shall be conclusive proof of proper substitution of such successor Trustee or Trustees, who shall, without conveyance from the Trustee predecessor, succeed to all its title, estate, rights, powers and duties. Said instrument must contain the name of the original Trustor, Trustee and Beneficiary hereunder, the book and page where this Deed is recorded and the name and address of the new Trustee.

(13) That this Deed applies to, inures to the benefit of, and binds all parties hereto, their heirs, legatees, devisees, administrators, executors, successors and assigns. The term Beneficiary shall mean the owner and holder, including pledgees, of the note secured hereby, whether or not named as Beneficiary herein. In this Deed, whenever the context so requires, the masculine gender includes the feminine and/or neuter, and the singular number includes the plural.

(14) That Trustee accepts under this Trust when this Deed, duly executed and acknowledged, is made a public record as provided by law. Trustee is not obligated to notify any party hereto of pending sale under any other Deed of Trust or of any action or proceeding in which Trustor, Beneficiary or Trustee shall be a party unless brought by Trustee.

2. The Promissory Note

The following promissory note is taken from Elias, *Make Your Own Contract* (Nolo Press), which explains in greater detail the choices you have when drawing up a promissory note.[6] This note allows for installment payments of the debt and includes interest. You can remove those provisions if you want the loan repaid all at once, in a lump sum, or if you don't want to charge interest.[7] A tear-out copy of the note is included in the Appendix.

PROMISSORY NOTE SECURED BY DEED OF TRUST

1. For value received,

    ☐ I individually
    ☐ We jointly and severally

promise to pay to the order of ___[person(s) to whom debt is owed]___
$ ____ at ____[address where payment is to be made]____ with interest at the rate of ___% per year:

[choose one]

    ☐ from the date this note is signed until the date it is due or is
       paid in full, whichever date occurs last.
    ☐ from the date this note is signed until the date it is paid in full.

2. The signer(s) of this note also agree that this note shall be paid in installments, which include principal and interest, of not less than $_____ per month, due on the first day of each month, until such time as the principal and interest are paid in full.

3. If any installment payment due under this note is not received by the holder within _____ days of its due date, the entire amount of unpaid principal shall become immediately due and payable at the option of the holder without prior notice to the signer(s) of this note.

---

[6]Like the other forms in this book, this promissory note should not be used in a commercial context. Special state and federal laws apply to notes used by businesses lending money to collect interest.

[7]*Make Your Own Contract* contains several promissory notes with different combinations of these terms. We include here the form we think most people will want to use when giving property as security for a loan.

4. In the event the holder(s) of this note prevail(s) in a lawsuit to collect on it, the signer(s) agree(s) to pay the holder(s)' attorney fees in an amount the court finds to be just and reasonable.

5. Signer(s) agree(s) that until such time as the principal and interest owed under this note are paid in full, the note shall be secured by a deed of trust to real property commonly known as   [address or other description] , owned by _____ [name] _____ executed on ___ [date signed] ___ at ___ [place signed] ___ and recorded on ___ [date recorded] ___ in the records of _____ County, California.

_____   _____
Date   Date

_____   _____
Location (city or county)   Location (city or county)

_____   _____
Name of Borrower   Name of Borrower

_____   _____
Address   Address

_____   _____

_____   _____
Signature of Borrower   Signature of Borrower

State of California
County of _____ } ss.

On _____19__, _____,
known to me or proved by satisfactory evidence to be the person(s) whose name(s) is/are subscribed above, personally appeared before me, a Notary Public for California, and acknowledged that _____ executed this note.

_____   [SEAL]
Signature of Notary

a. Identification of Parties

First, check the appropriate box, depending on how many people are signing the note. Remember that because of community property rules, spouses must sign notes secured by a deed of trust even if title to the property is in only one spouse's name (see Chapter 3, Section A). Then fill in the name and address of the lender and the amount the borrower is to pay back.

b. Interest Rates

Typical interest rates for family and personal debts range widely. In general, anything higher than 10% for personal and family loans violates the California usury (excessive interest) laws.[8] Although loans for the purchase of real estate may be exempt from the 10% limit, the law in this area is terminally confusing. Our advice is to stick to the 10% ceiling unless you check with a lawyer.

If you charge significantly less than the market rate, you should be aware that the IRS may treat the money the borrower is saving (compared to borrowing at the going rate of interest) as a gift. This is only a problem when the amount of money loaned is huge and the total gift exceeds the $10,000 annual federal gift tax exemption (see Chapter 2, Section C).

c. Prepayment Provisions

The first option does not allow credit for prepayment; the borrower must pay interest at the indicated rate for the entire loan period (and beyond if repayment is delayed). The second choice allows the loan to be prepaid, and interest is therefore only charged for the length of the time the loan is actually outstanding.

---

[8]Stats. 1919, § 5; Civil Code § 1916-2.

d. Amount of Installment Payments

Fill in the amount of the borrower's monthly payments. If no interest is being charged, figuring the amount of the payments is easy: just divide the amount of the loan by the number of months until it is due.

If interest is being charged, you need to consult the amortization schedule below. First, find the figure where the row with your interest rate and the column with the period of your loan intersect. To calculate the amount of the monthly payment, multiply that figure by the total amount of the loan.

Example: If your interest rate is 10% and the loan will be outstanding for five years, the figure from the amortization chart is 0.0212. Assuming a loan amount of $10,000, the monthly payments will each be .0212 x $10,000, or $212.

AMORTIZATION SCHEDULE

Years

	1	1 1/2	2	2 1/2	3	4	5	6	7	8	9	10
4 %	0.0851	0.0573	0.0434	0.0351	0.0295	0.0226	0.0184	0.0156	0.0137	0.0122	0.0110	0.0101
4 1/2 %	0.0854	0.0576	0.0436	0.0353	0.0297	0.0228	0.0186	0.0159	0.0139	0.0124	0.0113	0.0104
5 %	0.0856	0.0578	0.0439	0.0355	0.0300	0.0230	0.0189	0.0161	0.0141	0.0127	0.0115	0.0106
5 1/2 %	0.0858	0.0580	0.0441	0.0358	0.0302	0.0233	0.0191	0.0163	0.0144	0.0129	0.0118	0.0109
6 %	0.0861	0.0582	0.0443	0.0360	0.0304	0.0235	0.0193	0.0166	0.0146	0.0131	0.0120	0.0111
6 1/2 %	0.0863	0.0585	0.0445	0.0362	0.0306	0.0237	0.0196	0.0168	0.0148	0.0134	0.0123	0.0114
7 %	0.0865	0.0587	0.0448	0.0364	0.0309	0.0239	0.0198	0.0170	0.0151	0.0136	0.0125	0.0116
7 1/2 %	0.0868	0.0589	0.0450	0.0367	0.0311	0.0242	0.0200	0.0173	0.0153	0.0139	0.0128	0.0119
8 %	0.0870	0.0591	0.0452	0.0369	0.0313	0.0244	0.0203	0.0175	0.0156	0.0141	0.0130	0.0121
8 1/2 %	0.0872	0.0594	0.0455	0.0371	0.0316	0.0246	0.0205	0.0178	0.0158	0.0144	0.0133	0.0124
9 %	0.0875	0.0596	0.0457	0.0373	0.0318	0.0249	0.0208	0.0180	0.0161	0.0147	0.0135	0.0127
9 1/2 %	0.0877	0.0598	0.0459	0.0376	0.0320	0.0251	0.0210	0.0183	0.0163	0.0149	0.0138	0.0129
10 %	0.0879	0.0601	0.0461	0.0378	0.0323	0.0254	0.0212	0.0185	0.0166	0.0152	0.0141	0.0132

e. Acceleration Clause

This paragraph is a standard, though harsh-sounding, clause that allows the lender to declare the entire loan due if the borrower misses one payment by a certain number of days. That way, the lender can ask for the whole debt in one lawsuit. Otherwise, she would have to either bring a new suit every time a payment was missed (for the amount of that payment), or wait until all the installments should have been paid and then sue for the whole amount. Obviously, either of those options is impractical—hence the need for the acceleration clause.

f. Attorney's Fees

This provision makes the loser in a lawsuit responsible for the other side's attorney fees. Unless this clause is included, a small or medium-sized note is virtually uncollectible, because it costs more to collect it than it's worth. If for any reason you don't want to include this clause, just cross it out and have the borrower write her initials beside it.

g. Reference to Deed of Trust

Just as the deed of trust refers to the promissory note, the note refers to the deed of trust. Fill in the address of the property, the owners' names, and the dates and places the deed was signed and recorded.

h. Date and Signature

Here, the borrower (property owner) signs and dates the note.

i. Notarization

Unlike a deed, the signatures on a promissory note do not have to be notarized. However, since you've got to have the trust deed notarized anyway, we suggest that you go ahead and pay the nominal cost of having the note notarized too.

3. Delivery of the Deed

After the trust deed and promissory note have been filled out, signed, and notarized, you are ready to deliver the original deed to the beneficiary. Item 13 of Section B, Chapter 6 explains delivery. The borrower (trustor) should get a copy of the deed and note.

4. Checklist for Preparing a Trust Deed and Promissory Note

Does the trust deed:

• identify the trustor (borrower/property owner),

• identify the trustee (third party who will handle foreclosure if necessary),

• identify the beneficiary (lender for whom the property is security),

• describe the property accurately and completely, and

• refer to the promissory note evidencing the underlying debt?

Was the deed:

• signed by the trustor(s) (all owners of the property giving their interests as security, and their spouses),

• dated,

• notarized, and

• "delivered" to the beneficiary?

Does the promissory note:

• identify the lender and borrower,

• set out the terms of the loan: interest rate, monthly payments, length of the loan period, and

• refer to the deed of trust?

Was the note:

• signed and dated by the borrower (and spouse), and

• notarized?

The next step: After you've prepared the trust deed and promissory note, go to Chapter 7 for instructions on how to record the trust deed.

CHAPTER 6

PREPARING YOUR DEED

A deed is the document, signed by the person transferring real property, that actually transfers title to the property from one person (or business entity) to another. A valid written deed is the one absolutely essential element in a real estate change of ownership.[1]

The essential parts of all deeds are:

- Identification of the grantor (person making the transfer);
- Identification of the grantee (person receiving the deed);
- Words transferring the property;
- A description of the property being transferred; and
- Signature of the grantor.

Notarization isn't necessary for the validity of a deed, but it is required before you can record the deed with the county recorder.

---

[1]Actually, in some instances property may also be transferred by other documents, usually a court order.

Why isn't an oral agreement to transfer property enough? The short answer is because the law says it isn't. The idea behind the requirement of a formal, signed deed is to prevent confusion about who owns land. The goal of the whole system is to have a reliable and easily accessible written record of every transaction involving land. The crucial elements of the system are:

• a written deed, executed with enough detail and formality to make it reliable, and

• a recording system that keeps in one place, as public records, all deeds for land in a particular county (recording is discussed in Chapter 7).

"WITH THIS CLOD . . ."

Under early English common law, no documents were needed to transfer land, and no records were kept of transfers. In a society where most people stayed put, and most real property passed from father to eldest son, there was little need for either. To transfer land, the owner made the symbolic gesture of going to the property and handing the new owner a clod of dirt, a stone, or a stick. The little ceremony, done in front of witnesses, was called "livery of seisin"—feudal legalese for "delivery of title."

A deed is usually a simple one-page document. It's easy to prepare by filling in the blanks on the tear-out forms we provide. There are a few formalities, however, that must be followed to make a deed legally valid and fully effective. The owner (grantor) must formally "acknowledge" his signature on the deed (i.e., have it notarized) and "deliver" the deed to the new owner (grantee). The grantee should promptly record the deed with the county recorder.[2] There are also restrictions on who can deed property and rules about just what words should be used in the deed. The formalities surrounding deeds are another vestige of the tremendous importance English society placed on land transactions. Courts still take them quite seriously, however, and you should, too.

A. WHAT KIND OF DEED TO USE

So now you're ready to do what you set out to do—draw up a deed. How do you start? The first step is to choose, based on what you're trying to accomplish, among the different deed forms used in California. It's usually a very easy choice to make.

Three different kinds of deeds are used to transfer[3] land in California: grant, quitclaim, and warranty deeds. We include tear-out copies of grant and quitclaim deeds in the Appendix. We don't include a warranty deed, which is very rarely used. Let's look at each type in detail.

1. Grant Deeds

If you're transferring property outright, creating or changing ownership of co-owned property, or transferring property to or from a trust, you probably need a grant deed.

---

[2]The grantee isn't required by law to record the deed, but if he doesn't he runs the risk of serious complications later. See Chapter 7.

[3]If, instead of transferring the land, you want to give it as security for a debt, go to Chapter 5, which covers deeds of trust. Trust deeds do not really transfer ownership.

GRANT DEED

☒ This transfer is exempt from the documentary transfer tax.
☐ The documentary transfer tax is $_____ and is computed on
    ☐ the full value of the interest or property conveyed.
    ☐ the full value less the value of liens or encumbrances remaining thereon at the time of sale.
The property is located in ☐ an unincorporated area.☒ the city of __Pasadena__ .

For a valuable consideration, receipt of which is hereby acknowledged,

    ALEXANDER SINCLAIR and EMMA SINCLAIR, husband and wife,

hereby grant(s) to

    WALTER SINCLAIR and EVE SINCLAIR, as husband and wife,

the following real property in the City of __Pasadena__ , County of __Los Angeles__ , California:

    Portion of Lots 14 and 15, Block 3, of the Del Mar Tract, filed March 21, 1934, Map Book B, page 187, Los Angeles County records, described as follows:
    Beginning on the east line of Powell Street, distant thereon north 0° 45' west 59 feet from the southwest corner of Block 3; thence from the point of beginning north 0° 45' east along Powell Street 60 feet; thence southeast along the south line of Clay Street 113 feet to the point of beginning.
Date: ___July 19, 19__   _Emma Sinclair_
                                Alexander Sinclair

State of California
County of __Los Angeles__ } ss.

On __July 19, 19__ , __Emma Sinclair and Alexander Sinclair__ , known to me or proved by satisfactory evidence to be the person(s) whose name(s) is/are subscribed above, personally appeared before me, a Notary Public for California, and acknowledged that __they__ executed this deed.

___Kimberly Johnson___   [SEAL]
Signature of Notary

Recording requested by
WALTER SINCLAIR and EVE SINCLAIR
8714 Hayes Street
Pasadena, California 92408

and when recorded mail
this deed and tax statements to:

same as above

For recorder's use

A grant deed is the most commonly used kind of deed in California. It does the job for most transfers, especially intra-family transfers. For example, a grant deed is appropriate if you want to:

- transfer property you own yourself to someone else;

- transfer your interest as a co-owner to another co-owner;

- transfer property from a married couple to someone else;

- change the way co-owners hold title to property, e.g., from joint tenancy to community property or tenancy in common;

- transfer property to or from a trust; or

- transfer property to a custodian for a minor, under the Uniform Transfers to Minors Act.

Instructions for filling out a grant deed are in Section B below.

AFTER-ACQUIRED TITLE

If for some reason someone who executes a grant deed does not actually have title to the property, the grantee gets nothing, because the grantor had nothing to give. But if the grantor later acquires title, that "after-acquired title"[4] automatically passes to the grantee.

Example: Ed buys a house from Lorrie. Under the impression that Lorrie has signed a deed and sent it to him, Ed decides to put title jointly in his name and that of his wife. He executes and records a grant deed conveying the property to himself and his wife. Lorrie, however, changes her mind and doesn't sign or send the deed. The deed to Ed and his wife transfers nothing because Ed didn't own the property.

Later, Lorrie changes her mind again and sends Ed the deed. Under the rule of after-acquired title, Ed's wife also now owns a half-interest in the property.

This rule is not as arcane as it may seem. In times of ferment in the real estate market, investors and agencies often buy and sell many pieces of property in a short period of time. When the timing of the deals means that property is sold before the seller has clear title, the doctrine of after-acquired title helps clean up the mess.

---

[4]Civil Code § 1106.

2. Quitclaim Deeds

If you just want to release a possible claim to land—if, for example, you want to release a possible community property interest in property, clearing the way for your spouse or ex-spouse to sell or mortgage it—then use a quitclaim deed.

A quitclaim deed makes no promises whatsoever about the property interest being conveyed. Essentially, it means that the person who signs the deed is conveying whatever interest—if any—she has in the property. If the person does own the property, or an interest in it, the quitclaim deed is as effective to transfer ownership of that interest as a grant deed. If she doesn't own an interest in the property, the grantee has no recourse under the deed itself.[5]

As you might expect, a quitclaim deed is most useful when ownership of some parcel (or part of the parcel) of property is uncertain. It is commonly used when some person has a potential claim (often, a community property claim) to a piece of property that another person wants to sell. To avoid conflicts later, the person with the potential claim executes a quitclaim deed relinquishing all rights in the property.

If you are married and want to transfer property without your spouse's signature on the deed (or if you're divorcing and think you'll want to sell the property later), your spouse should execute a quitclaim deed giving her interest to you, even if you think your separate ownership of the property is perfectly clear. A bank or title company will insist on it. And even if a financial institution isn't involved in the current transaction, one is sure to be in on the act sometime in the future. Then, when the bank has the title checked and finds the transfer from only one spouse, it will undoubtedly insist on a quitclaim deed from the other spouse. It's easier to do it now than later. (See Chapter 3, Section A).

Example: Sue and Peter are getting divorced. They agree that Sue should keep the house. To ensure that Sue can prove, if she wants to sell or borrow against the house later, that it is really her separate property, Peter executes and records a quitclaim deed, giving to Sue any interest he might have in the house. When that's done, the public record will show title insurance companies, financial institutions, and potential buyers that Peter has no community property interest in the house.

---

[5]This does not necessarily mean the disappointed buyer can't sue the person who executed the deed; she may, depending on the circumstances, have an action for fraud or breach of contract.

Recording requested by
Susan E. Durant
8729 Marin
Berkeley, CA 94707

and when recorded mail
this deed and tax statements to:

same as above

For recorder's use

QUITCLAIM DEED

☒ This transfer is exempt from the documentary transfer tax.
☐ The documentary transfer tax is $_____ and is computed on
   ☐the full value of the interest or property conveyed.
   ☐the full value less the value of liens or encumbrances remaining thereon at the time of sale.
The property is located in ☐an unincorporated area. ☒the city of Berkeley   .

For a valuable consideration, receipt of which is hereby acknowledged,

   Peter S. Durant

hereby quitclaim(s) to

   Susan E. Durant

the following real property in the City of Berkeley   , County of Alameda   ,
California:

   Lot 7 of the Vernon Park Tract, filed May 17, 1964,
   in Book 48 of Maps, at page 132, in the Office of the
   County Recorder of Alameda County, California.

Date: February 3, 19 _____   _Peter S. Durant_____

                                   _____

                                   _____

                                   _____

State of California
County of _Alameda____) ss.

On _February 3, 19—_ , _PETER S. DURANT_____ , known to me or
proved by satisfactory evidence to be the person(s) whose name(s) is/are subscribed above, personally
appeared before me, a Notary Public for California, and
acknowledged that ___he___ executed this deed.

_____Mamie White._____   [SEAL]
Signature of Notary

Quitclaim deeds can also be used to settle uncertainty or disputes about other kinds of claims, including easements or rights to inherited property.

Example 1: Andy wants to sell his house to Bill, but Bill is reluctant to buy because Andy's next door neighbor, Marsha, has an easement that lets her use Andy's driveway to get to the back of her property. Andy explains the situation to Marsha, who is willing to give up the easement, which she seldom uses, for a payment of a few hundred dollars. She signs a quitclaim deed giving to Andy all rights (including the easement) she has in Andy's property, which means Bill can take the property free of her rights.

Example 2: Nathan's will was written ambiguously, so that it wasn't clear which of his daughters, or both, should inherit his house. The daughters, Lauren and Jane, settled the matter themselves, agreeing that Lauren should have the house and Jane should take some other property. As part of the settlement, Jane executes a quitclaim deed to Lauren, giving up any right she may have to the house.

After-acquired title note: The doctrine of after-acquired title (see Section 1 above) does not apply to quitclaim deeds, because someone who executes a quitclaim deed expressly transfers only whatever interest he has at the time. Thus if you receive a quitclaim deed from a person who doesn't actually have any interest in the property, and that person later does acquire some interest, you will not own that interest (unless a court finds some other doctrine that justifies giving it to you[6]).

Example: Michael executes a quitclaim deed to Sally. Sally records it and then discovers that Michael didn't have title to the land when he signed the deed, but got it the next day. Sally owns nothing; Michael still owns the property. He gave her (in the quitclaim deed) only the interest he had at that time, which was nothing.

Instructions for filling out a quitclaim deed are contained in Section C below.

---

[6]Courts have developed, over hundreds of years, doctrines that often give them considerable leeway in remedying an unfair result.

3. Warranty Deeds

A warranty deed, by which the grantor guarantees that he has good title to the property, is appropriate only when you want to custom-design your deed to take care of certain specialized problems with the transaction. We don't provide a warranty deed in this book.

A warranty deed contains express (not implied, as in the grant deed) promises about the title being transferred. Making those express promises about the title in a simple transfer is unnecessary and may cause complications later. It is unlikely that you will want to use a warranty deed in an intra-family transaction of the kind we discuss in this book

Warranty deeds are seldom used at all these days; their function has largely been taken over by title insurance, which guarantees that the grantor has good title to the property (see Chapter 2, Section D). Grantees usually prefer title insurance; with insurance, they are assured of getting back the money they paid for the property (from the insurance policy) if it turns out that someone else has a superior claim to the real estate. If, on the other hand, they have only the grantor's promise (and can only sue him), they may not be able to get their money back. With the spread of title insurance, about the only situation left where a warranty deed is useful is a commercial transaction, where the parties want to add their own special provisions and promises (termed covenants) to the deed.

B. PREPARING A GRANT OR QUITCLAIM DEED

Finally! You're ready to fill out your deed. You've done the hard part of the transfer procedure already by making all the decisions about how to take title and who should sign. All that's left is the mechanical process of filling in the blanks.

Tear-out blank grant and quitclaim deeds are included in the appendix of this book. You can use them or photocopies of them, or buy blank deed forms in many stationery stores. You can also draw up your own deed, but it's not advisable. Printed forms make things easier and help you avoid leaving out anything important.

DEED LANGUAGE
or
IS THIS ENGLISH?

Printed deed forms (the kind you get from the stationery stores) are given varying names. The most common titles are "Grant Deed" and "Quitclaim Deed." Others are headed "Joint Tenancy Deed." The important thing to know is that no matter what the title you have a grant deed, legally, any time the word "grant" is used in the deed itself. For example, a document that contains this language is a grant deed: "Jane Vanelli hereby grants to John Goodwin the following described property . . . ." The title of the deed itself makes no difference: the important thing is the language of transfer. Obviously, however, you shouldn't use a printed "Joint Tenancy Deed" unless you want to create a joint tenancy, simply because otherwise it's confusing.

The phrasing of form deeds also tends to be ridiculously formal and antiquated. It's still not uncommon to find grant deeds peppered with bold Gothic text proclaiming that the signer "grants, gives, bargains, sells, aliens, releases, enfeoffs, conveys, and confirms" his property to the new owner "to have and to hold." By the time you've read it all, you're not sure whether you're selling property or getting married. This excess language is at best unnecessary and at worst confusing. Our forms avoid it; if you're stuck with someone else's form, you can ignore it.

Language Note: California statutes (Govt. Code § 27293) require a deed to be written in English unless an English translation, certified accurate by a court, is attached.[7]

The following instructions are keyed to the sample deed shown below.[8] Preparing the deed isn't difficult, but pay attention to the details. It's worth taking a little time to do it right.

---

[7]The statute doesn't state whether or not the "legalese" most deeds are written in qualifies as English. We've got our doubts.

[8]If for some reason you find it necessary to write your own deed from scratch--we don't recommend it--at least type it. Courts and bureaucrats are used to typed documents, and it will be more readily accepted and less likely to be challenged.

Recording requested by

① _____

and when recorded mail
this deed and tax statements to:

② _____

For recorder's use

GRANT DEED

③

☐ This transfer is exempt from the documentary transfer tax.
☐ The documentary transfer tax is $_____ and is computed on
   ☐ the full value of the interest or property conveyed.
   ☐ the full value less the value of liens or encumbrances remaining thereon at the time of sale.
The property is located in ☐ an unincorporated area. ☐ the city of _____.

For a valuable consideration, receipt of which is hereby acknowledged,

  ④

hereby grant(s) to ⑤

  ⑥

the following real property in the City of _____, County of _____,
California:

   ⑦   ⑧   ⑨

Date: _____⑪_____   _____⑩_____

    _____   _____

    _____   _____

    _____   _____

State of California
County of _____ } ss.

On _____, _____⑫_____, known to me or
proved by satisfactory evidence to be the person(s) whose name(s) is/are subscribed above, personally
appeared before me, a Notary Public for California, and
acknowledged that _____ executed this deed.

_____   [SEAL]
Signature of Notary

1. Recording Information

The new owner has the responsibility for recording a deed with the county recorder, so her name goes in the "Recording Requested By" space. (Chapter 7 explains recording.)

2. Tax Statements

Property tax statements should be mailed to the new owner, so enter his name and address here. If there is more than one new owner, one name and address is sufficient. Be sure to fill this in; it is required by statute.[9] Some counties also require the tax roll parcel number of the property to be put on the deed. Find out by calling your county assessor or recorder. You can get the parcel number from an old property tax statement. Just type it in the margin of the deed. ("A.P.N." stands for "assessor's parcel number.")

3. Documentary Transfer Tax Information

The deed should state whether or not the transfer is subject to a local documentary transfer tax, which is levied when real property is sold and the deed is recorded (see Chapter 2, Section C).[10]

Gifts of real property and transfers between spouses dividing marital property are exempt from the tax. If your transfer is exempt from the tax, you should check the box in front of "This transfer is exempt from the documentary transfer tax" and attach a short signed statement that explicitly says why the transfer is exempt.

Gifts. Here is a statement you can use if the transfer is a gift[11] (a tear-out copy is in the Appendix):

---

[9]Govt. Code § 27321.5.

[10]Revenue & Taxation Code § 11911.

[11]Property put in a revocable living trust is exempt from documentary transfer tax because it is a gift. It is not a gift for federal gift tax purposes, however, because the transfer is revocable at any time.

DECLARATION OF EXEMPTION FROM DOCUMENTARY TRANSFER TAX: GIFT OF REAL PROPERTY

Grantor has not received and will not receive consideration from grantee for the transfer made by the attached deed. Therefore, under Revenue and Taxation Code Sec. 11911, the deed is not subject to the Documentary Transfer Tax.

I declare under penalty of perjury under the laws of California that the foregoing is true and correct.

_____
Grantor

Date:_____   _____, California

_____
Grantor

Date:_____   _____, California

Marital property division. To show why your transfer is exempt from the tax, one spouse (either one) should sign a declaration that states the transfer is made to divide community property between spouses in contemplation of divorce. This exemption does not apply to all transfers between spouses. Only if a court has issued a judgment or order dividing the property or the spouses, in contemplation of divorce, have signed a written agreement about how to divide property, is the transfer exempt. The appropriate reason should be checked on the declaration shown below. Here is a sample declaration; a tear-out copy is in the Appendix.

DECLARATION OF EXEMPTION FROM DOCUMENTARY TRANSFER TAX: DIVISION OF MARITAL REAL PROPERTY

The transfer made by the attached deed is made for the purpose of dividing community, quasi-community or quasi-marital real property between spouses, as required by:

☐ a judgment decreeing a dissolution of the marriage or legal separation, by a judgment of nullity, or by any other judgment or order rendered pursuant to Part 5 of Division 4 of the Civil Code, or

☐ a written agreement between the spouses executed in contemplation of such a judgment or order.

Therefore, under Revenue and Taxation Code Sec. 11927, the deed is not subject to the Documentary Transfer Tax.

I declare under penalty of perjury under the laws of California that the foregoing is true and correct.

_____

Grantor

Date:_____ _____, California

_____

Grantor

Date:_____ _____, California

If the transfer is subject to the tax, fill in the amount of the tax on the deed. You can find out the amount by calling the county recorder before you take in or mail the deed to record it. You must pay the tax (to the county recorder) before you can record the deed.

Counties are allowed to levy a documentary transfer tax of up to 55¢ per $500 (or part thereof) of the sale price (less the amount of any liens on the property, including deeds of trust, taken over by the new owner) when real property is sold. Some cities add taxes, so the actual rate may be much higher. In San Francisco, for example, the total rate is $5 per $1000.

The tax is figured on the value of the property transferred minus any liens remaining on it, so check the second box under the line with the amount unless there are no liens or encumbrances on the property.

Example: Hannah sells some property to her son, Nathan. The property is subject to a deed of trust and a tax lien. Hannah pays the tax lien before the transfer and Nathan takes responsibility for (assumes) the deed of trust. The documentary transfer tax will be figured on the value of the property minus the amount of the trust deed. On the deed, Hannah should check:

☐ *the full value less the value of liens or encumbrances . . .*

If Nathan were not taking the property subject to any liens or encumbrances, Hannah would check:

☐ *the full value of the interest or property conveyed.*

4. Identification of Grantor[12]

Here is where you fill in the names of all current owners of the property —the persons who will sign the deed.

If there is only one unmarried owner, it's good to add "an unmarried person" after his name to show that a spouse wasn't mistakenly left out of the document. When there is more than one owner, you should designate how they hold title now, like this: "Corrine W. Albertson and Ian R. Mayer, joint tenants." As discussed at length in Chapter 3, if any of the current owners are married, their spouses should sign the deed with them.

If there is a possibility of confusion about someone's name—for example, if the grantor took possession of the property under a different name than she is conveying it by—then all names must be included in the deed. This will make it clear that the different names refer to the same person and avoid the possibility of an apparent gap in the chain of title.

The easiest way to link the names is with "a.k.a." or "also known as." For example, if Maria Smith bought property but has since married and changed her name to Jones, the deed should identify her as "Maria Jones, a.k.a. Maria Smith."

---

[12]For brevity, we use "grantor" here when referring to anyone who's transferring property, by grant or quitclaim deed.

Under California law, if the name under which the grantor took title (the name on the earlier deed which transferred property to the grantor) is not included in the deed, the deed does not give later purchasers notice of the transfer, and the transfer is valid only between the parties and persons who have actual notice of it.[13] That is, later purchasers can't be expected to know about the transfer if it was made under a different name. For example, if Maria Jones neglects to add "a.k.a Maria Smith" to the deed, years later when a prospective buyer goes to the county recorder's office and looks up "Maria Jones" in the Grantor-Grantee Index (see Chapter 2, Section D), the earlier deed to Maria Smith won't appear.

5. Words of Transfer

The words of transfer, which show the grantor's intent to convey the property to the grantee, determine what kind of deed (grant or quitclaim) you have.

The deed forms in this book already have the correct word ("grant" or "quitclaim") printed on them. Don't get creative and add your own language to the deed to make it sound like one of those impressive store-bought ones that have a whole string of terms shoehorned into them. It may not hurt in most cases, but it sure doesn't help.

6. Identification of New Owner (Grantee)

The deed must clearly identify the grantee and how he, she, they or it (a trust, for example) is taking title. The pros and cons of the various ways to take title are discussed in Chapter 4. Here are examples of the choices for the actual wording of the deed:

To an unmarried recipient: "to Henry Anderson, an unmarried man."

To co-owners in joint tenancy: "to Henry Anderson and Melanie Strauss, in joint tenancy."[14]

To co-owners as tenants in common:

"to Henry Anderson and Melanie Strauss, as tenants in common."

---

[13]Civil Code § 1196.

[14]When personal property is put into joint tenancy, the title document often names the joint tenants as "X and Y, with right of survivorship" or abbreviated "X and Y, WROS" or "X and Y, JTWROS." With real property, however, it's almost always spelled out as in our example. To avoid confusion, do it like the example.

To a married couple as community property:[15]

1. "to Henry Anderson and Melanie Anderson, as community property," (this form is preferable) **or**

2. "to Henry Anderson and Melanie Anderson, as husband and wife."

To a living trust: "to Joan Goodman, in trust for Henry Anderson."

To a minor under the Uniform Transfers to Minors Act: "to Joan Goodman, as custodian for Henry Anderson until age 22, under the Uniform Transfers to Minors Act."

To a partnership: "to Elm Street Books, a partnership."

To a corporation: "to Anderson Enterprises, Inc., a California corporation."

Here are some special considerations:

• **Multiple grantees.** If you name more than one grantee, each is presumed to get an equal interest in the property unless the deed specifies different shares.

Example: A deed "to Reuben Gerber and Elizabeth Roman" gives each a half-interest in the property transferred.

Example: A deed "to Reuben Gerber, a one-third interest, and to Elizabeth Roman, a two-thirds interest, as tenants in common in the following described real property . . ." gives them unequal interests.[16]

It's allowable, but never advisable, to convey property to a class of persons—for example, "my children"—instead of naming each grantee. You're just asking for trouble, though. Even a seemingly simple term like "children" can cause confusion when stepchildren, adopted children, or out-of-wedlock children are involved. There's no reason not to name each person you want to own the property.

• **Persons who go by more than one name.** As mentioned in Section 4 above, if there is a chance that using only one name for a grantee will create confusion about his identity, spell out all names the grantee uses. For example, "Maria R. Smith, a.k.a. Maria Smith-Jones."

---

[15]Real property owned jointly by a husband and wife, no matter how title is held, is presumed to be community property if they divorce. See Chapter 4, Section C.

[16]Remember, tenancy in common is the only way to create unequal shares. Property held in joint tenancy must be shared equally by the co-owners.

7. Physical Description of the Property

Obviously, a deed must identify the property being transferred. Your description should start with the city (if the property isn't inside a city's limits, cross out "City of") and the county in which the property is located.

Next, on to the specific description. In almost every case you can simply copy the legal description from the old deed. If there isn't enough room on the deed to get the whole thing, type "See description on Attachment 1" in the space. Then either photocopy the old legal description or type it on a separate plain piece of paper, and label it, for example, "Attachment 1 to grant deed from Sonia O'Toole to Kyle Garrett, April 2, 1987," and staple it to the deed. To be extra careful, the grantor can sign the attachment page as well as the deed.

If you re-type the legal description (which may contain lots of strange-looking numbers and symbols), be very careful not to make a transcription error. Check it by having someone read out loud from the old deed while you follow along on the new one.

If the current owner can't find his deed, you should be able to get a copy of it from the county recorder's office (if, of course, it was recorded). If the recorder can't come up with a deed, this is a red flag—a possible break in the chain of title discussed in Chapter 2—warning you that something is very wrong. You should talk to someone at a title company or a lawyer.

You will need a new legal description if:

• you have reason to think that the old deed's description is erroneous; or

• you are transferring only part of the property described in the old deed.

In almost all cases, you will want to hire a surveyor or real estate profes-sional to help you with this. If you don't need to get a new description for your property, you can skip the rest of this section.

Order No. 49333 PC

EXHIBIT "A" AS REFERRED TO IN THE DEED FROM DAVID MACLEAN TO
REAL PROPERTIES, INC., a California corporation dated 9/17/84

The land referred to in this Report is situated in the State of California, County of Contra Costa
and is described as follows:
City of Richmond

Portion of Lots 11 and 13, Block 19, map of the San Pablo Villa Tract, filed September
21, 1905, Map Book C, page 65, Contra Costa County Records, described as follows:

Beginning on the east line of Mayes Street, formerly Powell Street, distant thereon
north 0 degrees 45' west 59 feet from the southwest corner of said Block 19; thence
from said point of beginning north 0 degrees 45' east along the east line of Mayes
Street 41.5 feet; thence southeasterly parallel with the south line of Emeric Avenue,
formerly Clay Street 112.5 feet to the west line of Lot 12; thence southerly along
said line 41.5 feet; thence northwesterly parallel with the south line of Emeric
Avenue 112.5 feet to the point of beginning.

BOOK 11983 PAGE 203

84 137602

END OF DOCUMENT

SCHEDULE A
CLTA Preliminary Report
1-1-84

Page 2 of 2

TITLE
GUARANTY COMPANY

There are four main ways property can be described, although no particular kind of description is required by statute. The general rule is that the description must be adequate to allow a surveyor to identify the land. It must, however, specify the county as well as the city; California statute (Civil Code § 1092) requires it.

(1) Metes and Bounds. The first method is called "metes and bounds," an old term meaning measures and directions. A metes and bounds description describes the perimeter of the property. The description must thus start at an identifiable point and end there as well. Here's an example that refers to a map recorded in San Francisco:

ORDER NO.   220-596-2

The land referred to in this Report is situated in the State of California, County of   City & SAN FRANCISCO, and is described as follows:

BEGINNING at a point on the northerly line of Geary Boulevard, formerly Geary Street, distant thereon 75 feet easterly from the easterly line of 44th Avenue; running thence northerly at right angles to said line of Geary Boulevard 90 feet, 1-1/4 inches to the southerly line of Point Lobos Avenue; thence easterly along said line of Point Lobos Avenue 31 feet, 10 inches; thence southerly 86 feet, 3/4 of an inch to a point on said northerly line of Geary Boulevard, distant thereon 92 feet, 4-3/8 inches easterly from the said easterly line of 44th Avenue; thence westerly along said line of Geary Boulevard 17 feet, 4-3/8 inches to the point of beginning.

BEING a portion of OUTSIDE LAND BLOCK NO. 224.

---

(2) Township/Range. The second way of describing property is based on a survey system that divides the state into a grid. The north-south lines are called ranges, and the east-west lines are called townships. The starting place for a description of this kind is always one of the three north-south lines in California that are designated as "principal meridians." The space on the grid where the property is located is identified by counting from a principal meridian. Each space on the grid east or west of a principal meridian counts as one range. Confused? It gets worse. Each space on the grid created by township and range lines is divided into 36 one-square mile sections. It's easier to understand by looking at a diagram:

TOWNSHIP/RANGE SYSTEM

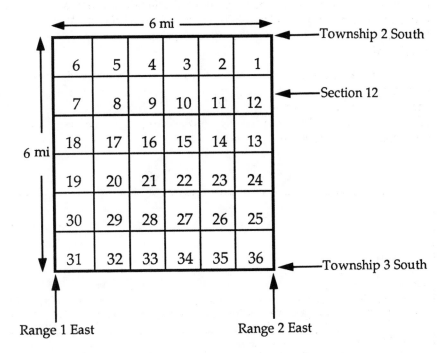

(3) Reference to a recorded map. The third way to describe property is much simpler and, of course, less common. It is simply a reference to an approved subdivision map or official city or county map that has been recorded with the county. The recorded map (also called a plat) will have the township and range coordinates on it.

Example: "Parcel 35 of Country View Estates, a duly recorded subdivision, a map of which was recorded in the Contra Costa County plat books at book 498, page 1213, on January 14, 1986."

(4) Name of the property. It is also permissible to refer to a piece of property by name, if it's generally known that way.[17] If, for example, you are trans- ferring the "Cartwright Ranch," and everyone will know what property that means, you're all right. Generally, though, you are better off to refer to a surveyor's description, either by including a metes and bounds or township/ range description or by referring to a recorded map. It's just more concrete and less likely to cause problems later on.

----

[17]Civil Code § 1092.

You may have noticed that none of these ways of describing land pays much attention to the number of square feet or acres in the property. If the number of acres is specified and doesn't agree with a more certain (e.g., metes and bounds) description, the more definite description prevails.

8. Encumbrances

As discussed in Section A above, unless a grant deed says otherwise, the law presumes that the interest transferred by these deeds is not encumbered (for example, by taxes, assessments, liens, or mortgages) except to the extent that the grantor has disclosed. Quitclaim deeds, on the other hand, only transfer whatever interest the grantor owns and are free of presumptions.

Accordingly, a grant deed should clearly identify all encumbrances. If it doesn't, the grantee can sue either for rescission (cancellation) of the sale or for the difference between what he paid for the property and its actual value taking into account the encumbrances.[18]

9. Covenants

When real property is transferred, restrictions on its use sometimes go with it. These restrictions, called "covenants running with the land," may be spelled out in the deed, but more commonly are recorded separately. Only covenants that relate to use of the property may run with the land. Examples are covenants to pay rent, to pay taxes, or to ensure "quiet enjoyment" of the property.[19] A covenant not related to the land—say, to belong to a certain church or give money to someone—will not be enforced.

Most people have no need to include covenants in a deed that simply transfers ownership within a family or changes the way title is held. These days covenants are most commonly used by homeowners' associations in

---

[18]Thus if the transfer was a gift, the grantee has no remedy.

[19]Civil Code §§ 1460 et seq.

subdivisions or condominium complexes. The grantee takes the property subject to a set of "conditions, covenants and restrictions," which is recorded in the Coumty Recorder's office. You can't eliminate these.

The restrictions can be quite detailed, covering everything from what color you can paint your house to what kind of fences, outbuildings, or pets you are allowed to have. Obviously, they can be quite important to anyone thinking of living there. Any prospective owner should get a complete copy of the restrictions, which the homeowner's association must provide upon request, before the transfer.

Racial covenants, which prohibited use of land by minorities, were shockingly common until the Supreme Court ruled them unenforceable in 1948.[20] They are now expressly prohibited by state statute.[21] Nonetheless, they persist in the records, impotent but ugly reminders of bigotry. Some deeds signed today still refer to covenants like this one, which is recorded in the Contra Costa County Recorder's office:

delivery of these presents, the receipt whereof is hereby acknowledged, has granted, bargained, sold and conveyed, and by these presents do grant, bargain, sell and convey unto said parties of the second part, and to their heirs and assigns forever,

ALL that certain real property, situate in the County of Contra Costa, State of California, and bounded and particularly described as follows, to-wit:

Lot Numbered Forty-three (43) as said lot is shown upon that certain map entitled, "Kensington Terrace, Contra Costa County, California, July 1926" - filed in the office of the County Recorder of the said County of Contra Costa, September 10, 1926 in Book 20 of Maps, at pages 519 and 520.

The property hereinabove described is conveyed and this deed is accepted pursuant to the following covenants, conditions and restrictions, which shall, as to each and every part thereof, apply to and be binding upon the said parties of the second part, their heirs and assigns, viz:

1. That no building other than a dwelling house shall be constructed upon the property herein described, and that no building used for dwelling purposes shall be constructed of a less vlaue than $3500.00, provided, however, that the usual garage and outbuildings may be constructed as appurtenant to said residence.

2. That neither said real property nor any interest therein nor any improvements thereon shall ever be used or occuped by any person of African, Mongolian, Chinese or Japanese descent, except as a servant of the then owner or occupant thereof.

---

[20]*Shelley v. Kraemer*, 334 U.S. 1 (1948).

[21]Covenants that directly or indirectly restrict the use or acquisition of property based on a person's sex, race, color, religion, ancestry, ethnic group or national origin are void. Civil Code §§ 53, 782.

If a legally enforceable covenant is violated, the injured party can sue the owner and collect money damages. The transfer of the property isn't affected; the grantor can't take the property back.

10. Signature of the Grantor

This one sounds, and usually is, straightforward enough. The important thing to remember is that all owners of the property being transferred, and their spouses, must sign the deed. The deed isn't binding on any who don't sign.[22] See Chapter 3 for the rules that govern who must sign the deed when a partnership or corporation transfers property.

Grantors should sign their names exactly as they are typed or printed on the deed.

Someone who has a written, recorded authorization to sign a deed for the owner (power of attorney) must both sign her name and include the name of the grantor, like this: "Ellen Palmer, attorney in fact for Sara Puchinsky." See Chapter 3, Section E.

Witnesses to the signing of the deed are not required, but notarization is a necessity (see Section 12 below if you want to record the deed).

11. Date

You should also put in the date each person signs the deed. The deed is effective only from the date of delivery (see Section 13 below), which is presumed to be the date of execution (signing).[23]

---

[22]It is possible, though seldom desirable, for one co-owner to transfer only his interest in real property; in that case, only that owner would sign. See Chapter 3.

[23]If the co-grantors sign on different dates, the important date is probably the latest date.

12. Acknowledgment (Notarization)

The acknowledgment of the grantor's signature on a deed is formal proof that the signature is genuine. The grantor states, before a notary public, that he is the person whose signature appears on the deed, and the notary signs a statement to that effect. Notarization has nothing to do with the substance of the deed or the grantor's title to the property being transferred.

As mentioned notarization of the signature on a deed is not required for the deed's validity. As long as you sign a deed that contains all the elements set out above, the deed is legal and binding on the parties. Acknowledgment, however, is required if you want to record your deed with the county recorder—which you do (take our word for it—Chapter 7 discusses the recording system). We include the mechanics of completing the notarization here for convenience, because you will want to fill out the acknowledgment part of the deed when you sign it. After the deed is signed and notarized, go to Section E.

a. If the Grantor Is in California

A notary public can acknowledge a signature anywhere in the state. You can usually find a notary in a bank, real estate agency, or lawyer's office. Other public officials can acknowledge a signature in the county or city in which they are elected or appointed: a municipal or justice court judge or clerk, county or city clerk, court commissioner, district or city attorney, county counsel, or clerk of a board of supervisors.[24]

b. If the Grantor Is Outside California

If the grantor is outside the state, she can have her signature verified by a notary public for the state she is in, or by anyone else authorized by that state to take acknowledgments. If the grantor is outside the country, certain diplomatic personnel and foreign judges and notaries may take the acknowledgment.[25]

---

[24]Civil Code § 1181.

[25]Civil Code § 1183 provides that, outside the country, acknowledgment or proof of a deed may be made before: a minister, commissioner, or charge′ d'affaires of the United States, resident and accredited in the country where the proof or acknowledgment is made; a consul, vice consul, or consular agent of the United States, resident in the country where the proof or acknowledgment is made; a judge of a court of record of the country where the proof or acknowledgment is made; commissioners appointed by the Governor or Secretary of State for that purpose; or a notary public. If a notary public takes the acknowledgment, the notary's signature must itself be acknowledged before a judge or American diplomatic or consular officer.

Wherever the grantor is, she should use the acknowledgment form approved by California (the one on the form deeds in this book). Otherwise a California county recorder may not want to accept the deed for recording.

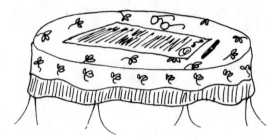

c. If the Grantor Is in the Armed Services

There are also special rules for members of the Armed Services. Officers who have the powers of a notary public can notarize documents for any service members, in the United States or out; outside the country, they can also notarize documents for spouses of persons serving in the Armed Forces or employees of the services.

FORM FOR ACKNOWLEDGMENT: MILITARY PERSONNEL

On this the _____ day of _____, 19___, before me, _____, the undersigned officer, personally appeared _____, known to me (or satisfactorily proven) to be (a) serving in the armed forces of the United States, (b) a spouse of a person serving in the armed forces of the United States, or (c) a person serving with, employed by, or accompanying the armed forces of the United States outside the United States and outside the Canal Zone, Puerto Rico, Guam, and the Virgin Islands, and to be the person whose name is subscribed to the within instrument and acknowledged that he executed the same. And the undersigned does further certify that he is at the date of this certificate a commissioned officer in the active service of the armed forces of the United States having the general powers of a notary public under the provisions of Section 936 of Title 10 of the United States Code (Public Law 90-632).

_____

_____
Signature of officer and serial number, rank,
branch of service and capacity in which signed.

---

d. If Acknowledgment Is Impossible

If for some reason you have a deed that cannot be acknowledged by the grantor himself—if, for example, the grantor signed the deed years ago but never acknowledged it and is now unavailable—you may still be able to record the deed by following one of the procedures below. (If the grantor can acknowledge the deed, you can skip this section).

(1) Witnesses

In rare instances, the signing of the deed may have been witnessed. A witness who signed the deed may execute a document proving that the person whose name is signed to the deed as grantor actually signed the deed and that the witness also signed the deed.

(2) Handwriting verification

If no witnesses are available, proof of the execution of the deed may be made by verification of the handwriting of the grantor. Witnesses and parties are considered unavailable if they are nonresidents of California, if they cannot be found or if they refuse to testify.[26]

To prove the grantor's handwriting, someone must sign a statement to the effect that he knew the grantor and his handwriting (and the witnesses who signed the deed, if any, and their handwriting) and that the signature is genuine. Like an acknowledgment, this statement must be made before a notary public or one of the other persons authorized by statute.

[26]Civil Code § 1198.

Here is a sample statement:

AFFIDAVIT

I, Jonathan Goldman, hereby state that I knew the late Julia Buckley for eight years and am very familiar with her handwriting. During the time I knew her I received numerous documents from her with her signature and saw her sign checks and other documents.

Based on my familiarity with Ms. Buckley's handwriting, I believe that she signed the deed to Fred Cohen, a copy of which is attached.

_____   _____
Date

State of California
County of _____ } ss.

On _____,19__, _____, known to me or proved by satisfactory evidence to be the person whose name is subscribed above, personally appeared before me, a Notary Public for California, and acknowledged that _____ executed this document.

_____   [SEAL]
Notary Public

---

13. Delivery of the Deed

A deed doesn't take effect unless it is delivered to and accepted by the grantee. This is a formal, not physical, requirement; usually the parties to a transaction need do nothing special to effect delivery (and in fact, it's likely that nine out of ten of them are blissfully unaware of the requirement). It's one of the silliest aspects of the relentlessly abstruse law of real estate. Basically, the law considers a deed delivered if the parties agree when the deed is signed that it is delivered, even if it is not actually in the grantee's possession.

Here are the technical rules. Delivery is, essentially, any act that indicates the intent to make the conveyance. It is not equivalent to physical delivery of the deed itself. Acts indicating the intent to transfer include recording the deed or physically delivering it to the grantee.

Delivery to an agent of the grantee, or to someone acting with the grantee's permission, is also sufficient (Civil Code § 1059). Delivery to one joint owner is sufficient.

A deed is presumed to have been delivered on the date it is properly executed (Civil Code §§ 1054, 1055). This presumption applies only to the date, not the fact, of delivery—that is, if the deed was in fact delivered, the statute presumes that the date of delivery is the date the deed was signed.

C. CHECKLIST FOR PREPARING A GRANT OR QUITCLAIM DEED

Does the deed

- contain required tax and recording information,
- identify the grantor(s) (and their spouses),
- identify the grantee(s),
- have the right words of transfer ("grant" or "quitclaim"), and
- describe the property accurately and completely?

Was the deed

- signed by the grantor(s) and their spouses,
- dated,
- notarized, and
- "delivered" to the grantee?

D. REVOKING A DEED

A deed is irrevocable. If you change your mind after you sign and deliver a deed, you're out of luck. On the bright side, this means that if you lose a recorded deed, there's no problem except inconvenience. You can get a certified copy from the county recorder.

If the person you transferred the property to agrees to transfer it back to you or to someone else, she must execute a new deed complying with the same formalities as the first one. Making an oral agreement, or just tearing up a deed that has been recorded, has no legal effect.[27]

---

[27] Of course, if you sign a deed but don't tell the grantee about it, and tear it up, no transfer was made. Similarly, if you have retrieve possession of deed which has been delivered but not yet recorded, and tear it up, the deed is effectively cancelled. In practical terms, the real point of no return is either when the deed is recorded or when it is retained by the grantee after being physically delivered.

If you transferred the property to a revocable living trust, you can revoke the trust and have the trustee (who may be yourself) transfer the property back to you.

CHAPTER 7

RECORDING YOUR DEED

Once you've completed the right deed for your transfer, you should be able to relax, right? Absolutely not. You still should record the deed with the county recorder. But take heart—recording is the last hoop you have to jump through when you're dealing with a real estate transaction, and it's not at all difficult.

Important: Any document (not just deeds) that may affect the title to real property should be recorded. For example, an agreement between a married couple as to the community property status of real estate owned by one or both of them, an affidavit of death of a joint tenant, or a power of attorney that gives the attorney in fact authority to sign deeds, should be recorded.

The mechanics of recording are outlined in Section B below. If you want an overview of the rationale and functioning of the recording system, read Section A first.

A. THE REAL PROPERTY RECORDING SYSTEM

The recording system is designed to keep track, in public records, of who owns every square inch of land in California. It's administered by each county, but the rules come from state statutes. They require each county to have a county recorder's office, where copies of all deeds (and other documents affecting title) to property in the county are collected and indexed. Usually, deeds are indexed by name of the owners (all parties to a deed—grantors and grantees—are indexed), so you have to look up a specific person instead of the property.

Keeping these records of all property transfers in one place allows (at least in theory) a prospective buyer to find out just who owns property, how much it is mortgaged for, and if it is subject to any other encumbrances or restrictions (a trust deed or lien, for example). The whole idea is to have one place, the county recorder's office, where buyers can look up their property and be sure they have found all documents that affect title to it.[1]

Here, in summary, are the rules of the system:

1. If a deed (or other document affecting title) is not recorded, it is not binding on someone who buys the property later with no knowledge of the earlier deed or document.

2. If a deed (or other document affecting title) is recorded, the law presumes that everyone in the world has notice of the document. Thus if you buy property that is subject to a recorded easement, you are deemed to know about the easement even though you may not actually know of it.

1. How the Recording System Works

As just stated, the law considers you to have knowledge (notice) of everything in the public records dealing with your property whether or not you've actually looked at them. Obviously, if someone doesn't record a transfer of title

---

[1]Usually, professional title searchers do the looking. Title searches and title insurance are discussed in Chapter 2, Section D.

(or easement, etc.), the public records will be inaccurate, and someone relying on them will be misled.

To protect persons who buy property in reliance on county records, the law provides that an unrecorded transfer is not binding on third parties who buy (or lend money when the property is used as collateral) in good faith without knowledge of the transfer. In other words, if someone who doesn't know of a previous transfer (because it wasn't recorded) relies on county records (which don't show the transfer) she is protected—it's as if the unrecorded transfer never happened.

Example: Ruth gives her house to her daughter Vera, but Vera doesn't record the deed. Later Ruth changes her mind and sells the house to Ray, who doesn't know about the previous deed to Vera (it wasn't recorded and he didn't find out any other way). When Ray records the deed, he is the legal owner of the property; his deed takes precedence over Vera's.

What about the validity of the transfer itself? Recording doesn't affect that; an unrecorded transfer is valid as to the parties directly involved and anyone who has knowledge of the transaction.

Example: Kim sells a piece of property to Mark. Robin knows about the sale but also knows that Mark hasn't recorded the deed. She buys the same property from Kim and runs down to record her deed first. She gets to the County Recorder before Mark does. Mark's deed still stands. The recording statute does not protect Robin, who bought the property knowing that it had already been sold to someone else.[2]

2. Persons Not Protected By Recording

The theory behind the recording scheme is that only someone who invests a substantial sum of money, in the honest belief that he is getting good title to property, should be protected. The recording statutes do not protect persons who acquire property without paying something for it.

Example: Ellen sells her farm to her neighbor, Myrtle. Myrtle doesn't get around to recording the deed until after Ellen executes and records another deed giving the farm to her son, Ross. Myrtle's deed, though recorded later, still takes precedence over Ross's, because Ross, who received the property as a gift, isn't protected by the recording laws.

The statute also does not, in most cases, help creditors who obtain a court judgment in a lawsuit against the former owner of the property.[3] As discussed above, the statute protects only persons who buy property without knowledge of

---

[2]Kim may also be in trouble. It's a criminal offense to sell, with the intent to defraud, the same piece of land twice. See Penal Code § 533.

[3]If your property is affected by a lawsuit, you should see a lawyer.

an earlier deed.

Example: Phoebe sells a piece of land to Hillary, but Hillary doesn't record the deed. Phoebe then defaults on a loan. The creditor obtains a court judgment and gets an order allowing him to satisfy the debt out of the property transferred to Hillary. Hillary then records the deed and protests that she owns the land. Under the recording statutes, the creditor is out of luck, even though he had no way of knowing that Phoebe didn't still own the property when he sued her.[4]

Note: The fact that the county recorder accepts a deed for recording does not mean it's valid.. For instance, a forged deed would not be made valid by recording.

B. HOW TO RECORD YOUR DEED

Recording a deed really is a simple process, but you need to do more than just take your deed to the county recorder's office. Before the recorder will accept your deed for recording, you must pay the documentary transfer tax, if applicable (see Chapter 6, Section C) and file a change of ownership report. We discuss these steps below.

---

[4]This example assumes that Phoebe didn't fraudulently get the creditor to extend her credit based on her ownership of the property and then transfer it to Hillary to avoid paying her debt. Fraudulent transfers of land are dealt with by another statute, Civil Code § 3439.04. They aren't discussed in this book.

1. Prepare Change of Ownership Forms

Two distinct forms, confusingly titled "Preliminary Change of Ownership Report" and "Change in Ownership Statement," exist to notify local property tax assessors of real estate transfers that may require a reassessment for tax purposes.[5] All transfers require the "preliminary" form, which must be filed when the deed is recorded. Some other transfers also require the second form; it is filed after recording. We discuss it in this chapter (subsection b below) for convenience.

a. Preliminary Change of Ownership Report

All documents that reflect a transfer of real property must be accompanied by a "Preliminary Change of Ownership Report" when they are recorded.[6] The recorder takes the form and sends it on to the assessor. If you don't turn it in with the deed, you are liable for an extra $20 fee (unless the new owner is not a California resident) and will have to fill out and file a "Change in Ownership Statement."

Each county has its own form, although the information requested is exactly the same. You can get copies from the recorder's office or the county assessor's office.

The form asks for basic information about the property and the transfer. Item 1 asks a series of questions to determine if the transfer is a "change of ownership," as defined by statute, making it subject to reappraisal by the county assessor for property tax purposes.[7]

If the transfer falls into any of the categories listed in Item 1, it is exempt and you need not fill in any of the detailed transfer information (sales price, loan information, etc.) that is asked for on the rest of the form. If it is not exempt, you will have to fill out the rest of the preliminary form.

This form should be easy to fill out after reading this book. If you have questions, check the earlier discussions of ways of holding title (Chapter 4) and tax reassessment (Chapter 2, Section 3), or ask the clerk at the County Recorder's Office.

---

[5]All information you supply on the forms is confidential; the county will not disclose it or make it a public record. Revenue & Taxation Code § 481.

[6]Revenue & Taxation Code § 480.3.

[7]Property tax reassessment is discussed in chapter 2, Section C.

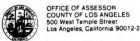

OFFICE OF ASSESSOR
COUNTY OF LOS ANGELES
500 West Temple Street
Los Angeles, California 90012-2770

PRELIMINARY CHANGE OF OWNERSHIP REPORT

(To be completed by transferee (buyer) prior to transfer of the subject property in accordance with Section 480.3 of the Revenue and Taxation Code.)

THIS SPACE FOR RECORDER'S USE

Seller/Transferor	Buyer/Transferee	Assessor's Identification No. (s) Mapbook - Page - Parcel Number
Legal Description: Tract Block Lot	Address (City, State, Zip)	**FOR ASSESSOR'S USE ONLY**
Mail Tax Information to: Name No. Street City State , Zip		Cluster _____ OC1 _____ OC2 _____

The property which you acquired may be subject to a supplemental assessment in an amount to be determined by the OFFICE OF ASSESSOR. For further information on your supplemental roll obligation, please call the OFFICE OF ASSESSOR at (213) 974-3211.

DT _____ INT _____
RC _____ SP $ _____
DTT $ _____ # Pcl _____

1. TRANSFER INFORMATION:

A. Was this transfer solely between husband and wife, addition of a spouse, death of a spouse, a divorce settlement, etc.?   a. ☐ YES   b. ☐ NO

B. Was this transaction only a correction of the name(s) of the person(s) holding title to the property?   a. ☐ YES   b. ☐ NO

C. Was this document recorded to create, terminate, or reconvey a lender's interest in the property?   a. ☐ YES   b. ☐ NO

D. Was this transaction recorded to create, terminate, or reconvey a security interest (e.g., co-signer)?   a. ☐ YES   b. ☐ NO

E. Was this document recorded to substitute a trustee under a deed of trust, mortgage, or other similar document?   a. ☐ YES   b. ☐ NO

F. Did this transfer result in the creation of a joint tenancy in which the seller (transferor) remains as one of the joint tenants?   a. ☐ YES   b. ☐ NO

G. Does this transfer return property to the person who created the joint tenancy (original transferor)?   a. ☐ YES   b. ☐ NO

H. Is this transfer of property:

a. to a trust for the benefit of the grantor?   a. ☐ YES   b. ☐ NO
b. to a revocable trust?   a. ☐ YES   b. ☐ NO
c. to a trust from which the property reverts to the grantor within 12 years?   a. ☐ YES   b. ☐ NO

I. If this property is subject to a lease, is the remaining lease term 35 years or more, including written options?   a. ☐ YES   b. ☐ NO

J. If this transfer is excluded from a change in ownership as defined in Section 62 of the Revenue and Taxation Code for any reason other than those listed above, set forth   the specific exclusion

claimed:_____   a. ☐ YES   b. ☐ NO

_____

IF YOU HAVE ANSWERED "NO" TO QUESTIONS "A" THROUGH "I", INCLUSIVE, AND HAVE NOT CLAIMED ANY OTHER EXCLUSION UNDER "J", PLEASE COMPLETE THE BALANCE OF THIS FORM. OTHERWISE, SIGN AND DATE ON THE REVERSE SIDE.

2. TYPE OF PROPERTY TRANSFERRED:

A. ☐ Single-family residence
B. ☐ Multiple-family residence (no. of units: _____)
C. ☐ Co-op
D. ☐ Condominium
E. ☐ Mobilehome
F. ☐ Unimproved lot
G. ☐ Commercial/Industrial
H. ☐ Other (description) _____

OWN-70 (Rev. 2/27/85)   Side 1

3. PURCHASE PRICE INFORMATION

A. Cash Downpayment or Value of Trade (excluding closing cost). ....Amount $_____

B. 1st Deed of Trust at _____% Interest for _____ years ....Amount $_____

☐ Fixed Rate
☐ New Loan
☐ FHA
☐ Cal-Vet
☐ VA
☐ Bank
☐ Balloon Payment ☐ YES. Amount $_____   ☐ NO

☐ Variable Rate
☐ Assumed Existing Loan Balance
☐ Finance Company
☐ Savings and Loan
☐ Loan Carried by Seller
☐ All Inclusive

C. 2nd Deed of Trust at _____% Interest for _____years ....Amount $_____

☐ Fixed Rate
☐ New Loan
☐ Loan Carried by Seller
☐ Balloon Payment ☐ YES Amount $_____   ☐ NO

☐ Variable Rate
☐ Assumed Existing Loan Balance

D. Was other type of financing involved not covered in (B) or (C) above?   ☐ YES   ☐ NO

Type _____ at _____% Interest for _____ years. ....Amount $_____

☐ Fixed Rate
☐ New Loan
☐ Loan Carried by Seller
☐ Balloon Payment ☐ YES Amount $_____   ☐ NO

☐ Variable Rate
☐ Assumed Existing Loan Balance

E. Improvement Bond: ☐ YES   ☐ NO
   Outstanding Balance..Amount $_____

F. **TOTAL PURCHASE PRICE** (or Acquisition Price, if exchanged) **ADD A THROUGH E**..............Amount $_____

ADDITIONAL QUESTIONS

4. Was any personal property included in the purchase, other than a mobilehome, subject to local property tax?   a ☐ YES   b. ☐ NO
   If yes, enter amount and attach itemized list of personal property.   Amount $ _____

5. Transfer is by:
   A. ☐ Deed   B. ☐ Contract of sale
   C. ☐ Foreclosure   D. ☐ Other--Explain _____
      Instrument

6. Was only a partial interest in the property transferred? ....a ☐ YES   b. ☐ NO
   If "YES" indicate the percentage transferred. _____%

7. A. ☐ Date of Transfer _____(if same as recording date, enter "See Recording Date"); or
   B. ☐ If an Inheritance, Date of Death _____

8. Is, or will, the property (be) producing income? ....a ☐ YES   b. ☐ NO

9. If answer to Question 8 is "YES", is income pursuant to:
   A. ☐ Lease   B. ☐ Contract
   C. ☐ Mineral Rights D. ☐ Other--Explain_____

0. Did the transfer of this property involve the trade or exchange of other real property?...............a ☐ YES   b. ☐ NO

1. Is this property intended as your principal residence?...a ☐ YES   b. ☐ NO

   If "YES", enter date of occupancy_____(if same as recording date, enter "See Recording Date")

   or intended date of occupancy _____

I certify that the foregoing is true, correct and complete to the best of my knowledge and belief.

Signed _____   Date_____
       (New Owner/Corporate Officer)

Telephone number where you are available from 8:00 a.m. - 5:00 p.m. ( )_____

(Note: The Office of Assessor may contact you for further information.)

If a document evidencing a change of ownership is presented to the recorder for recordation without the concurrent filing of a PRELIMINARY CHANGE OF OWNERSHIP REPORT, the recorder may charge an additional recording fee of twenty dollars ($20). The additional fee shall not be charged if the document is accompanied by an affidavit that the transferee is not a resident of California.

AFFIDAVIT OF NON-RESIDENT TRANSFEREE

The Transferee (buyer) named above is a resident of_____and not a resident of the State of California.
                                                        (State)
Signed _____   Date: _____
       (New Owner Corporate Officer)
                                    Side 2

b. Change in Ownership Statement

A Change in Ownership Statement, which is handled by the county assessor's office (not the county recorder) is required only when the property must be reassessed for property tax purposes or if you don't turn in a Preliminary Change in Ownership Report.[8] The assessor decides, based on the information in the Preliminary Report, whether or not you need to file one. If you do, the assessor will mail you a form. You don't need to worry about it unless you are sent one.

Many intra-family transfers of the type discussed in this book do *not* require a Change in Ownership Statement. The discussion of property tax reassessment in Chapter 2, Section C lists types of transfers that are not considered a "change in ownership" and thus do not require a Change in Ownership Statement or property tax reassessment.[9]

Like the preliminary form, this form varies slightly from county to county. The information it asks for is similar to that requested on the Preliminary Change of Ownership Report. Again, if you have questions, re-read the discussions of title and taxes in Chapters 2 and 4, or ask the clerks in the County Recorder's office for help

You will have 45 days (from the date it's mailed to you) to file the Change in Ownership Statement without penalty. The penalty for late filing is a fine of either $100 or 10% of the taxes on the new assessed property value (up to $2500), whichever is greater.

2. Take the Deed and Tax Statements to the Recorder

After your deed is properly drawn up, signed, and acknowledged (notarized), and the Preliminary Change of Ownership Report has been filled out, the person receiving the property should immediately take (or mail) them to the county recorder's office for the county in which the land is situated. You must take the signed original of the deed for recording.

In many counties, the recorder's office is in the county courthouse. (Two notable exceptions: in Los Angeles it's in the Hall of Records; in San Francisco it's in City Hall.)

---

[8]Revenue & Taxation Code § 480.

[9]Revenue & Taxation Code § 62. Some other transfers also do not require a Change in Ownership Statement; we list only the situations that are covered in this book.

From The Office Of
SAM DUCA, Assessor
City and County of San Francisco
Room 101, City Hall
San Francisco, California 94102

CHANGE IN OWNERSHIP STATEMENT
REAL PROPERTY OR MOBILEHOMES SUBJECT TO
LOCAL PROPERTY TAXES

Correct mailing address if necessary

Name and Address of Buyer/Transferee *(Last name, first name(s), initial)*

┌

└

Seller/Transferor _____
(Last name, first name(s), initial)

FOR INFORMATION CALL:

RECORDING DATA

Date _____

Document No. _____

Book _____ Page _____

ASSESSOR'S IDENTIFICATION NUMBER

VOLUME	BLOCK	LOT

Property Address _____

**PLEASE ENCLOSE A COPY OF
REAL ESTATE CLOSING STATEMENT**

Legal Description _____

IMPORTANT NOTICE

SECTION 480 OF THE CALIFORNIA REVENUE AND TAXATION CODE REQUIRES ANY TRANSFEREE ACQUIRING AN INTEREST IN REAL PROPERTY OR MOBILEHOME SUBJECT TO LOCAL PROPERTY TAXATION TO FILE A CHANGE IN OWNERSHIP STATEMENT WITH THE COUNTY RECORDER OR ASSESSOR. THE CHANGE IN OWNERSHIP STATEMENT MUST BE FILED AT THE TIME OF RECORDING OR, IF THE TRANSFER IS NOT RECORDED, WITHIN 45 DAYS OF THE DATE OF THE CHANGE IN OWNERSHIP. THE FAILURE TO FILE A CHANGE IN OWNERSHIP STATEMENT WITHIN 45 DAYS FROM THE DATE OF A WRITTEN REQUEST BY THE ASSESSOR RESULTS IN A PENALTY OF ONE HUNDRED DOLLARS ($100) OR 10 PERCENT OF THE CURRENT YEAR'S TAXES ON THE REAL PROPERTY OR MOBILEHOME, WHICHEVER IS GREATER. THIS PENALTY WILL BE ADDED TO THE ROLL AND SHALL BE TREATED AND COLLECTED LIKE, AND SHALL BE SUBJECT TO THE SAME PENALTIES FOR DELIN-QUENCY AS, ALL OTHER TAXES ON THE ROLL ON WHICH IT IS ENTERED.

This notice is a written request from the Office of Assessor for a Change in Ownership Statement. Failure to file this statement results in the assessment of a penalty. This statement will be held secret as required by Section 481 of the Revenue and Taxation Code.

A | **REAL PROPERTY CHANGE IN OWNERSHIP TRANSFER INFORMATION.** *Check (✓) all appropriate boxes*
"YES" or "NO" to indicate the method by which you acquired an interest in the property.

YES NO

1. ☐ ☐ PURCHASE

2. ☐ ☐ LAND SALES CONTRACT — a contract for the purchase of property in which the seller retains legal title to it after the buyer takes possession.

3. ☐ ☐ INHERITANCE — Transfer by will or as required if no will.
Date of Death _____
Relationship to Deceased _____

4. ☐ ☐ TRADE OR EXCHANGE — The above described property has been traded or exchanged for other real property or tangible or intangible personal property.

5. ☐ ☐ LEASE WITH A TERM OF 35 YEARS OR MORE — Creation, assignment, or termination of a lease or sublease with a term of 35 years or more (including renewal options).

6. ☐ ☐ MERGER OR STOCK ACQUISITION

7. ☐ ☐ PARTIAL INTEREST TRANSFER — Was only a partial interest in the property transferred? If "YES" indicate the percentage transferred. _____ %

8. ☐ ☐ Was this transfer solely between husband and wife, addition of a spouse, death of a spouse, divorce settlement, etc.)

YES NO

9. ☐ ☐ Was this transaction only a correction of the name(s) of the person(s) holding title to the property?

10. ☐ ☐ If you hold title to this property as a joint tenant, is the seller or transferor also a joint tenant?

11. ☐ ☐ Was this transaction the termination of a joint tenancy interest?

12. ☐ ☐ Was this a transfer between family members or related businesses?

13. ☐ ☐ Was this document recorded to substitute a trustee under a deed of trust, mortgage, or other similar document?

14. ☐ ☐ Was this document recorded to create, assign, or terminate a lender's interest in this property?

15. ☐ ☐ Has this property been transferred to a trust? If "YES" is the trust: ☐ Revocable   ☐ Irrevocable

16a. ☐ ☐ If the trust is irrevocable, is the transferor or the transferor's spouse a present beneficiary?

16b. ☐ ☐ Does this property revert to the transferor in 12 years or less? (Clifford Trust)

If you have answered "YES" to 16a or 16b, attach a copy of the trust agreement to this statement.

PLEASE COMPLETE THE REVERSE SIDE

ENCLOSE A COPY OF REAL ESTATE CLOSING STATEMENT

SBE-ASD AH 502 FRONT 7-21-80 (REVISED 9-30-80)

B **PROPERTY INFORMATION** *Complete each item as it applies to this transaction. Enter "N/A" (Not Applicable) if an item does not apply. Attach or explain any additional information in Remarks (Section D) below.*

1. **Type of Property**
   - ☐ Single Family Residence
   - ☐ Condominium or Co-Op
   - ☐ Multi-Family
   - ☐ Railroad or Public Utility
   - ☐ Unlicensed Mobilehome
   - ☐ Commercial or Industrial
   - ☐ Agricultural
   - ☐ Residential Lot
   - ☐ Vacant Land
   - ☐ Other _____

   DESCRIBE

2. Does this property produce income from a mineral lease? ☐ YES ☐ NO
3. Does this property produce income from sources other than mineral leases? ☐ YES ☐ NO
   If you have answered "YES" to either question 2 or 3, please attach a current income and expense statement.
4. If the property is subject to a lease, state its original term (including options and the beginning date of the lease) _____
   _____
5. If an improvement bond was included under the purchase/transfer agreement enter its amount on Line 4(d) below in the loan amount column (If none, so state.)
6. If personal property was included in the purchase price, attach an itemized listing of the personal property and enter its value $ _____
   Personal property includes, but is not limited to, licensed mobilehomes and unattached items such as furniture, appliances, and movable equipment (everything except land and permanent structures).

C **PURCHASE PRICE OR TRANSFER AMOUNT INFORMATION** *Complete each item as it applies to this transaction. Enter "N/A" if an item does not apply. Explain all terms of this transaction.*

1. Date you signed agreement to purchase the property	2. Date you took title (usually recording date)	3. Is this property your principal residence? ☐ YES ☐ NO

4. **Financing**

   (a) **CASH DOWN PAYMENT** $ _____ – Do not include closing costs (loan fees, title, escrow, taxes, etc.)

NEW LOAN / ASSUMED LOAN	LOAN AMOUNT	TERM (IN YEARS)	INTEREST RATE (%)	SOURCE OF FINANCING: Bank, Savings and Loan, VA, FHA, Insurance Co., Other	AMT. OF POINTS	LOAN DISCOUNT PAID BY BUYER	SELLER
(b) ☐ ☐ 1st $ _____	_____	_____	_____	_____	_____	☐	☐
(c) ☐ ☐ 2nd $ _____	_____	_____	_____	_____	_____	☐	☐
(d) ☐ ☐ Other $ _____	_____	_____	_____	_____	_____	☐	☐

   TOTAL PURCHASE PRICE $ _____   OR INDICATED VALUE FOR THE PROPERTY $ _____

D **REMARKS** *Please attach or explain below any additional information about the sale or transfer which should be called to the attention of the Office of Assessor.*

The Office of Assessor may contact you for additional information regarding this transaction.
I declare under penalty of perjury that the foregoing is true and correct to the best of my knowledge and belief.

Signed in _____, California, this _____ day of _____ 19____.

SIGNATURE OF OWNER OR CORPORATE OFFICER	TITLE, IF CORPORATE OFFICER/PARTNER	TELEPHONE (8 AM – 5 PM

RETURN COMPLETED STATEMENT TO: Room 101, City Hall San Francisco, CA 94102

SBE-ASD AH 502 BACK 7-31-80 REVISED 9-30-80

If your transaction is subject to the documentary transfer tax, a local tax assessed on property sales, you must pay the tax when the deed is recorded. You should have determined, when you filled out your deed using Chapter 6, Section B, the amount of tax due. Deeds of trust and some transfer deeds are exempt from the tax.

You will also have to pay a small recording fee. Current fees are about $5 for the first page and $2 for each additional page.

The clerk in the recorder's office will take your original deed, stamp it with the date and time, a filing number, and book and page numbers, make a copy, and give the original back to you. That's it. Filing numbers are given sequentially. The book and page numbers show where the copy of the deed will be found in the county's records, which are now on microfilm in most counties. Recording is effective the minute the clerk accepts your deed.

OFFICIAL RECORDS COUNTY OF MARIN

Order No.   138565-RH
Escrow No. N-150926-MN
Loan No.

86 59788

RECORDED AT REQUEST OF

TITLE CO.

1986 OCT 24 AM 8 00

OFFICIAL RECORDS
MARIN COUNTY CALIFORNIA

WHEN RECORDED MAIL TO:

Mr. and Mrs. James Chadwick
495 Oxford Circle
Greenbrae, CA 94904

SPACE ABOVE THIS LINE FOR RECORDER'S USE

MAIL TAX STATEMENTS TO:

DOCUMENTARY TRANSFER TAX $ 240.90
XX
___ Computed on the consideration or value of property conveyed; OR
___ Computed on the consideration or value less liens or encumbrances remaining at time of sale.

Same as above

FIRST AMERICAN TITLE CO.
Signature of Declarant or Agent determining tax – Firm Name
FIRST AMERICAN TITLE COMPANY

#70-162-02
Tax Code Area 68-004

GRANT DEED

FOR A VALUABLE CONSIDERATION, receipt of which is hereby acknowledged,

ROBERT J. TILLSON and WILMA MAE TILLSON, husband and wife

Recording by mail. Mailing in your deed for recording (with a check for the fees and taxes) is perfectly permissible and can save you lots of time. But before you send off your deed, call the recorder's office and check on fees and documentary transfer taxes.

If you mail the original deed, you should keep at least one photocopy. You should also include a cover letter (a sample letter is shown below) and a stamped, self-addressed envelope so the recorder can return the original of the deed to you. Whether or not you want to trust your deed to the mails is up to you. Certified mail is probably smart, although if you're going to have to stand in line at the post office you may decide it's easier just to go to the recorder's office.

SAMPLE COVER LETTER FOR RECORDING DEED

James Ferguson
1485 Lafayette St.
Inglewood, CA 98807

February 6, 19____

County Recorder
227 North Broadway
Los Angeles, CA 90012

   Enclosed for recording is a deed transferring real property located at 1230 Lafayette Street, Inglewood, in Los Angeles County. Also enclosed are a Preliminary Change in Ownership Report and a check in the amount of $5.00 to cover the recording fee. As noted on the deed, the transfer is exempt from the documentary transfer tax (Rev. & Tax. Code § 11911).

   Please record the deed and return it to me in the enclosed stamped, self-addressed envelope. Thank you.

                              Sincerely,

                              James Ferguson

Note on time limits: If a deed severing a joint tenancy (see Chapter 3) is executed by only one joint tenant, it must be recorded before that joint tenant's death to defeat the survivorship interests of the remaining joint tenants. The only exception is if the deed is executed fewer than four days before the death of the joint tenant; in that case, it may be recorded up to a week after the death and still terminate the other joint tenants' right of survivorship.[10]

There are no other legal time limits for recording. You can record a deed at any time after it's acknowledged, but it obviously makes sense to record it as soon as you can. Delay invites the confusion and trouble that the recording system was set up to avoid (see Section A above).

C. RECORDING CHECKLIST

Before you mail or take your deed to the county recorder's office, make sure you have:

- completely filled out the deed;
- signed the deed and had the signature notarized;
- made a photocopy for each party to the transaction;
- checked the recording fees;
- determined how much, if any, documentary transfer tax you must pay; and
- filled out a Preliminary Change in Ownership Report.

If you mail the deed, enclose:

- the original (signed) deed;
- a check for recording fees;
- a check for the documentary transfer tax, if applicable;
- a stamped, self-addressed envelope so the recorder can return the original deed to you; and
- the Preliminary Change of Ownership Report.

Afterward, be sure to notify the holder of any mortgage of the new owner's name and address, and fill out the Change in Ownership Statement if the assessor sends you one.

---

[10]Civil Code § 683.2.

C H A P T E R 8

WHEN YOU NEED AN EXPERT

Sometimes, whether you're fixing your car, building a deck or dealing with real estate, you have to admit you need an expert's help. When it comes to real property, sometimes even the most determined self-helper may need to consult an accountant, a real estate broker, or one of those pin-striped characters with the briefcases. At several points throughout the book we've suggested that you see an expert if you find yourself in certain situations, including:

- a dispute over ownership of property;
- uncertainty about estate planning or federal gift or income tax questions;
- an apparent gap in the title to the property;
- doubt about the proper way to hold title in your situation; or
- a complicated community property problem.

A. WHERE TO GO FOR HELP

Before you go off in search of an expert, here are some tips:

• **Real estate brokers**, who work in the field day in and day out, may have the answer you need at their fingertips. Many are willing to consult with you for a fee, on an hourly basis.

• **Title company employees** and clerks in county recorder's and assessor's offices may be able to assist you with questions about real estate transfers. Often your question may be a simple one that has more to do with local custom than a legal technicality.

• **A tax accountant** is usually the best source of up-to-date information about gift or income taxes.

• **A lawyer** will probably be needed if there is a dispute over ownership of the property or if you have a serious community property problem. If you decide to see a lawyer, keep in mind that hiring a lawyer does not mean giving up control of whatever task it is that you want to accomplish. You do not have to turn your problem over to a lawyer who will "take care of it" and send you a bill. Your goal should probably be to consult a lawyer on specific questions that come up as you transfer real estate or handle any other routine legal matter yourself. And after reading this book, you should be familiar enough with the concepts and terminology of real estate law to confidently pose your questions.

B. ACCOUNTANTS

People who have never worked with a certified public account (CPA) who has tax experience are often unsure of how to begin. Many seem to believe that hiring an accountant means calling a huge national accounting firm. In fact, finding a competent local accountant to advise you on tax questions should be easy. Usually, your best bet is to ask small businesspersons you know for a recommendation. Once you get a few names, give them a call and outline your problems. Ask what they charge and if they have had experience with your kind of situation.

C. LAWYERS

As we mentioned, many real estate problems don't require the help of an attorney. Before you decide you need to hire a lawyer, make sure you really have a legal question—not just a question about how things are customarily handled at the county recorder's office or by a title company.

1. Finding a Lawyer

Especially in California, locating a lawyer is no problem. Their advertisements shout from billboards, television, radio, and newspapers, and the yellow pages are full of listings. But finding a knowledgeable lawyer who charges reasonable rates, is willing to give you advice in discrete bits, and whom you trust is not always easy. Picking a name out of the phone book is a common but obviously unreliable method.

Castles in the air are the only property you can own without the intervention of lawyers. Unfortunately, there are no title deeds to them.

—J. Feidor Rees

Referral panels set up by bar associations are also not high on our list of favorite ways to find a lawyer. They're hardly more reliable than the yellow pages. Although lawyers are sometimes listed by specialty, they are rarely screened in any meaningful way. Often the referral panels are just a haven for inexperienced lawyers who need business.

Unquestionably, the best way to find a good attorney is to get a recommendation from a friend. People who run small businesses are likely to have consulted a lawyer; ask them who they see and what it costs. They may also know if their attorneys are knowledgeable about real estate law. Attorneys, like everyone else, have become more and more specialized; a lawyer who does personal injury trial work may not have looked at a deed in years.

When you get a couple of prospects, call the law offices and outline your problem to the attorney. Explain that you just want to get some questions answered and ask how much an initial consultation will cost. When you find someone you feel comfortable with, make an appointment.

2. Lawyers' Fees

Lawyers' rates range from $50 to $300 per hour; $90-$150 per hour is common. We believe it's smarter to pay this rate for all consultations with the lawyer, including the first visit, even though some lawyers offer a free short consultation to attract new clients. If you go in for a free initial consultation, you put the lawyer in the position of not making (or even losing) money unless she sells you some services. It's far better to find, and pay, a busy, experienced lawyer who doesn't need to schedule "happy hours" for new clients.

Especially if you go to one of the advertised legal clinics, make sure you understand what is included in the price you are quoted. Clinics sometimes advertise a low price for a particular service and then add to it if your problem has any complications whatsoever. Be wary when dealing with the heavily-advertised clinics.

Other clinics, set up with the public interest in mind, may be more helpful. For example, in northern California, Consumer's Group Legal Services in El Cerrito provides good, affordable services and supports the idea of its members helping themselves as much as they can. Membership and hourly consultation fees are reasonable.

If you see an attorney in private practice, one who has a reasonably simple office and lifestyle is more likely to help you for a reasonable cost than is a lawyer who has an elaborate office and a $750 suit. (Just remember that his clients paid for the suit.)

D. DOING LEGAL RESEARCH YOURSELF

It's always possible to use some of the lawyers' tools without using the lawyers. You can find information on California real estate law at any law library. Every county has a law library (in the courthouse), and usually a law librarian will be happy to help you. Law school libraries are also generally open to the public. A complete guide to legal research, showing you everything from what the books look like to how to research a complicated problem, is *Legal Research: How To Find and Understand the Law,* by Stephen Elias (Nolo Press).

One of the main resources for real estate problems is the California Civil Code (cited frequently throughout this book), which contains most of the statutes that govern deeds and land transfers. Another good way to start is to look under "deeds" in a legal encyclopedia for California called California Jurisprudence (usually abbreviated as Cal Jur).

A useful and readable book is *Real Estate Law in California,* by Bowman and Milligan (Prentice-Hall Co., 7th ed. 1986). Also helpful are publications on real estate that are aimed at lawyers but can be used fairly easily by lay-persons. One example is *California Real Estate Law and Practice* , a multi-volume reference work published by Matthew Bender Co. The California Department of Real Estate publishes *Real Estate Law,* another helpful book.

GLOSSARY

Note: For a much more extensive glossary, see the *Dictionary of Real Estate Terms* (Barron's), available through Nolo Press.

Acceleration clause: In a promissory note, a clause that allows the lender to declare the entire amount of the loan due if the borrower misses one payment. Without an acceleration clause, the lender would either have to bring a new lawsuit every time a payment is missed or wait until all payments, over the entire period of the loan, were due. Due-on-sale clauses, which make entire real estate loans due if the property is sold, are also referred to as acceleration clauses.

Acknowledgment: A written statement on a deed, made by the person who signs the deed and witnessed by a notary public, that the signature on the deed is valid.

After-acquired title: Title to property that is acquired by someone after that person has purportedly transferred title to it to someone else. Under the law, as soon as the seller actually acquires title, it passes to the person he purported to transfer it to before.

ALTA (American Land Title Association) title insurance policy: A title insurance policy, usually purchased (in the amount of the loan) by a lender financing a real estate purchase, that covers more than the standard (CLTA) policy.

A.P.N. (Assessor's Parcel Number): The designation of property on the local property tax rolls. Some counties require the A.P.N. to be put on deeds that are recorded.

Basis: The figure from which profit on the sale of property is computed for income tax purposes. For example, if your basis in your house is $50,000, and you sell it for $75,000, you make a profit of $25,000. The basis is usually what you paid for the property or its value when you inherited it, subject to certain adjustments for capital improvements and other factors.

Beneficiary: A person who inherits under a will or receives property put in trust. Under a deed of trust that secures a loan, the beneficiary is the lender.

Bequest: A gift made in a will.

Capital improvements: Permanent improvements that increase the value of your property and have a useful life of more than a year--for example, new insulation or a new patio. Ordinary repairs and maintenance don't qualify as capital improvements.

Chain of title: The line of owners of real property, stretching back in time from the current owner to the original grant from some government (in California, often the Spanish government, in the 19th century). An error in this chain of title is what title searches are supposed to find and what title insurance protect you against.

Change in Ownership Statement: A form that asks for infomation relating to property taxation, which must be filed with the county assessor in certain kinds of real estate transactions. If the form is required, the assessor will send it to the new owner.

CLTA (California Land Title Association) title insurance policy: The standard form for title insurance in California, usually bought by someone who is buying real property.

Community property: Very generally, all property acquired by a couple during marriage and before permanent separation, except for gifts to and inheritances by one spouse only. The nature of the property (community or separate) can be changed by written agreement between the spouses. See **separate property.**

Conservator: Someone appointed by a court to manage the affairs of a mentally incompetent person.

Consideration: The legal term for something given in exchange for property. Deed forms often say the grantor is transferring property "for good and valuable consideration, receipt of which is hereby acknowledged . . . ." It just means that the grantor got something in exchange for the property.

Corpus: The Latin word for the property held in a trust.

Covenant: A promise. Promises in deeds are usually called covenants.

Covenants, Conditions and Restrictions (CC&R's): Restrictions that govern the use of real property. They are usually enforced by a homeowners' association, and must be passed on the new owners of the property. If your

association, and must be passed on the new owners of the property. If your property is subject to CC&R's, you must disclose this to the buyer before title is transferred.

Custodian: A person appointed under the Uniform Transfers To Minors Act to manage property for a minor.

Deed: A document that transfers ownership of real property. See **grant, quitclaim** and **warranty.**

Dissolution: The legal term for divorce.

Documentary transfer tax: A tax imposed by cities and counties on sales of real estate. The total charged cannot be more than 55¢ per $500 of the sales price. The tax must be paid before the deed can be recorded.

Donor: A person who makes a gift.

Due on sale clause: A provision in a mortgage or promissory note that makes the entire amount of a real estate loan due when the property is sold. Also called an acceleration clause.

Easement: A legal right to use another's land, usually for a limited purpose. For example, you can grant someone an easement to use a corner of your property as a shortcut to their property. An easement is a legal interest in land, and the written grant of an easement should be recorded. When real property is transferred, a recorded easement goes with it; the new owner takes the property subject to the easement.

Emancipated minor: A minor who has the rights of an adult because he has been married, is in the military, or has been declared emancipated by a court.

Encumbrance: An interest in real property owned by another, such as a lien, mortgage, trust deed, or other claim, which impedes the transfer of title to the land.

Equity: The value of an owner's interest in real property. Calculate equity by subtracting the value of any deeds of trust or other encumbrances from the total value of the property.

Escrow: The process during which a buyer and seller of real estate deposit documents and funds with a third party (the escrow holder, which is usually an escrow or title company) with instructions for making the transfer. To close escrow, the company transfers the buyer's money to the seller and transfers the deed to the property to the buyer.

Fee simple: An old term meaning complete ownership of real property. An owner with a fee simple has no restrictions, inherent in the way he holds title, on his right to transfer the property during his life or leave it by his will. The title may, in reality, have encumbrances that make it harder to transfer; that's another issue.

Fixture: Something that is permanently attached to real property and is considered part of the real property. For example, bookshelves built into a house are fixtures; free-standing bookshelves are considered furniture, not part of the real property. Unless otherwise specified in a sale contract, fixtures are transferred with the real property.

Foreclosure: The forced sale of real property, ordered by a court or under a trustee's power of sale, to pay off a loan that the owner of the property has defaulted on.

Gift tax: The Federal Unified Gift and Estate Tax is imposed when someone gives away valuable property while he is alive or leaves it at his death. Up to $600,000 of property may be given away tax-free. If any tax is due, it is usually paid only after the person has died.

Grant: The transfer of title to real property by deed or some other document.

Grant deed: A deed that uses the word "grant" and implies certain promises by the grantor about the title to the property. This is the most commonly used kind of deed.

Grantee: The recipient of a grant of real property.

Grantor: The person who signs a deed granting real property to another person or entity.

Heir: A person who inherits property that is not disposed of in a will or trust. A decedent's heirs are determined by statute.

Incumbrance: See encumbrance.

Joint tenancy: A way co-owners may hold title to property so that when one co-owner dies, her interest in the property passes directly to the surviving co-owners without probate and regardless of any will provision to the contrary. Compare **tenancy in common.**

Legal description: A description, in a deed, of the location of land, sufficiently detailed to enable a surveyor to identify the property.

Lien: A claim on property for payment of a debt. For example, a tax lien is a lien placed on property when the owner has not paid taxes. A mechanic's lien is imposed by someone who makes improvements on the house (a carpenter, for example). If the carpenter isn't paid, he can enforce his claim by foreclosing on the property. See Civil Code § 3110.

Life estate (life tenancy): An interest in land that is measured by someone's lifetime. The holder of a life estate has the use of the real estate for his lifetime (or, rarely, for the lifetime of someone else) only. When the life estate ends, ownership of the property goes to someone else already chosen by the original owner of the property.

Lis pendens: A notice, recorded in the county recorder's office, of a pending lawsuit that affects title to the land. It gives notice to anyone who is thinking of buying the property that there may be a problem with the current owner's title to the property.

Minor: In California, someone who is less than 18 years old.

Partition: A court-ordered sale or division of jointly owned property. Any co-owner may petition the superior court for a partition order.

Partition: A court-ordered sale or division of jointly owned property. Any co-owner may petition the superior court for a partition order.

Personal property: All possessions that aren't considered real estate (see **real property**).

Power of attorney: Authority to act on another person's behalf. For example, if you will be out of town when your property sale is likely to take place, you can give someone (a co-owner, most likely) the authority to sign the deed for you. A **conventional power of attorney** terminates if the principal becomes incapacitated; a **durable power of attorney** does not.

Preliminary Change of Ownership Report: A form that must be filed with the county recorder whenever real estate changes hands.

Probate: The time-consuming and often expensive process in which a court supervises the transfer of a decedent's estate to his heirs and beneficiaries. The necessity for probate can be avoided if property is held in certain forms of ownership, such as joint tenancy, community property or trusts.

Promissory note: A written promise to pay money.

Property taxes: Local taxes imposed annually on real estate.

Quasi-community property: Property acquired by a married couple while living outside California that would have been community property had the couple been living in California.

Quitclaim deed: A deed that transfers any ownership interest the person signing it may have in particular property but does not guarantee anything about the extent of that interest.

Real Estate Transfer Disclosure Statement: A detailed disclosure form, which a seller is required by law to fill out and give to the buyer before title is transferred. The form covers the condition of the property.

Real property (real estate): Land and things permanently affixed to land, such as buildings.

Recording: The process of filing a copy of a deed with the County Recorder for the county in which the land is located. Recording creates a public record of all changes in ownership of all property in the state.

Remainder: The legal term for the property interest that's left over after someone is given a less than complete interest in land. For example, when someone is given a life estate, the rest of the ownership interest (that is, ownership after the holder of the life estate dies), is called the remainder and must also belong to someone.

Right of survivorship: The right of a surviving joint tenant to take ownership of a deceased joint tenant's share of the property.

Security interest: A claim against property, given by a debtor to ensure payment of a debt. For example, if you borrow money, you may execute a deed of trust on your house, giving the lender the right to have the house sold to pay the debt if you don't pay back the loan. The lender has a security interest in your house.

Separate property: Property that is not community property; that is, property that is acquired by an unmarried person or acquired by gift or inheritance by a married person.

Settlor: One who sets up a trust (same as **trustor**).

Special studies zones: Areas of possible earthquake hazards, delineated by state geologists. Sellers must tell buyers if the property is located within a special studies zone.

Tenancy by the entirety: A way for married couples to hold title to property. It is no longer used in California, although some statutes still refer to it.

Tenancy in common: A way for co-owners to hold title that allows them maximum freedom to dispose of their interests by sale, gift, or will. Upon a co-owner's death, his share goes to his beneficiaries (if there is a will) or heirs, not to the other co-owners. Compare **joint tenancy.**

Title: Evidence of ownership of real property.

Title company: A company that conducts title searches, issues title insurance and often handles escrow proceedings.

Title insurance: Insurance that guarantees a buyer against defects in the title of the real property being bought--that is, that no one besides the title holder has any claim to the property.

Title search: A search of the public records in the county recorder's office, usually made by a title insurance company, to see if the current owner of real property actually has good title to the land and that no challenges have been raised.

Trust: A device by which title to property is transferred to a person called a trustee, who manages the property for the benefit of another person called a beneficiary. The person who sets up the trust is the trustor or settlor. Trusts can be living (*inter vivos*), which means set up while the trustor is alive, or testamentary, which means set up in the trustor's will. Living trusts are usually revocable, but they can be made irrevocable.

Trust deed: In California, the most common instrument for financing real estate purchases (many other states use mortgages). The trust deed transfers title to land to a trustee, who holds it as security for a loan. When the loan is paid off, title is transferred to the borrower. The trustee has no powers unless the borrower defaults on the loan or violates one of the other promises in the trust deed; then the trustee can sell the property and pay the lender back from the proceeds.

Trustee: A trustee for a living or testamentary trust manages trust property for a beneficiary. The trustee named in a trust deed does not exercise any control over the property; he has only the power to sell the property if the trust deed is defaulted on.

Trustor: One who sets up a trust for someone else (this term has largely been replaced by the term **settlor**).

Uniform Transfers To Minors Act: A set of statutes adopted by the California legislature that provides a method for transferring property to minors by allowing the giver to appoint a "custodian" to manage the property for the minor.

Usury: The charging of an illegally high rate of interest on a loan. In California, 12% annual interest is the ceiling for private loans. Ten percent is the top rate for "personal and household" loans, but loans to purchase real estate are not considered personal loans. As is obvious to anyone who has a credit card, banks are allowed to charge much more.

Warranty deed: A seldom-used kind of deed, which contains certain express promises about the title being transferred.

APPENDIX

Grant Deed

Quitclaim Deed

Deed of Trust

Promissory Note Secured By Deed of Trust

Real Estate Transfer Disclosure Statement

Special Studies Zone Disclosure form

Form for Acknowledgment: Military Personnel

Declaration of Exemption from Documentary Transfer Tax: Gift of Real Property

Declaration of Exemption from Documentary Transfer Tax: Division of Marital Real Property

Recording requested by

and when recorded mail
this deed and tax statements to:

For recorder's use

GRANT DEED

☐ This transfer is exempt from the documentary transfer tax.
☐ The documentary transfer tax is $_____ and is computed on:
    ☐ the full value of the interest or property conveyed.
    ☐ the full value less the value of liens or encumbrances remaining thereon at the time of sale.
The property is located in ☐ an unincorporated area. ☐ the city of _____.

For a valuable consideration, receipt of which is hereby acknowledged,

hereby grant(s) to

the following real property in the City of _____, County of _____,
California:

Date: _____   _____

         _____   _____

         _____   _____

         _____   _____

State of California
County of _____} ss.

On _____19__, _____,
known to me or proved by satisfactory evidence to be the person(s) whose name(s) is/are subscribed
above, personally appeared before me, a Notary Public for California, and acknowledged that
_____ executed this note.

                                            [SEAL]

_____
Signature of Notary

For recorder's use

DEED OF TRUST

_____, Trustor(s), hereby grants
_____, Trustee, with power of sale, the
following real property in the City of _____, County of _____, California:

together with its rents, issues and profits, subject to the Beneficiary's rights to collect and apply rents, issues and profits, given by paragraph 10 of the provisions of the fictitious deed of trust incorporated herein by reference.

This deed is executed to secure payment of the debt evidenced by a promissory note signed by Trustor(s) _____, 19___ in favor of_____, Beneficiary, in the sum of $_____.

Trustor agrees that by execution and delivery of the deed of trust and the note it secures, provisions one through 14 of the fictitious deed of trust recorded October 18, 1961 in Santa Barbara and Sonoma Counties and in all other counties October 23, 1961, as set out below, are adopted and incorporated herein and that Trustor will observe those provisions.

The fictitious deed of trust incorporated herein is recorded with the county recorder of each California county as follows:

COUNTY	BOOK	PAGE	COUNTY	BOOK	PAGE	COUNTY	BOOK	PAGE	COUNTY	BOOK	PAGE
Alameda	435	684	Kings	792	833	Placer	895	301	Shasta	684	528
Alpine	1	250	Lake	362	39	Plumas	151	5	Sierra	29	335
Amador	104	348	Lassen	171	471	Riverside	3005	523	Siskiyou	468	181
Butte	1145	1	Los Angeles	T2055	899	Sacramento	4331	62	Solano	1105	182
Calaveras	145	152	Madera	810	170	San Benito	271	383	Sonoma	1851	689
Colusa	296	617	Marin	1508	339	San Bernardino	5567	61	Stanislaus	1715	1456
Contra Costa	3978	47	Mariposa	77	292	San Francisco	A332	905	Sutter	572	297
Del Norte	78	414	Mendocino	579	530	San Joaquin	2470	311	Tehama	491	289
El Dorado	568	456	Merced	1547	*538	San Luis Obispo	1151	12	Trinity	93	366
Fresno	4626	572	Modoc	184	851	San Mateo	4078	420	Tulare	2294	275
Glenn	422	184	Mono	52	429	Santa Barbara	1878	860	Tuolumne	135	47
Humboldt	657	527	Monterey	2194	538	Santa Clara	5336	342	Ventura	2062	386
Imperial	1091	501	Napa	639	86	Santa Cruz	1431	494	Yolo	653	245
Inyo	147	598	Nevada	305	320	San Diego	Series 2	Page	Yuba	334	486
Kern	3427	60	Orange	5889	611		Book 1961	183887			

A copy of any Notice of Default and any Notice of Sale under this deed of trust shall be mailed to Trustor(s) at:

_____

_____

Date:_____   _____

Signature of Trustor

Date:_____   _____

Signature of Trustor

State of California
County of _____ } ss.

On _____ 19___, _____,
known to me or proved by satisfactory evidence to be the person(s) whose name(s) is/are subscribed above, personally appeared before me, a Notary Public for California, and acknowledged that _____ executed this deed.

[SEAL]

_____

Signature of Notary

The following is a copy of provisions (1) to (14), inclusive, of the fictitious deed of trust, recorded in each county in California, as stated in the foregoing Deed of Trust and incorporated by reference in said Deed of Trust as being a part thereof as if set forth at length therein.

To Protect the Security of This Deed of Trust, Trustor agrees:

(1) To keep said property in good condition and repair; not to remove or demolish any building thereon; to complete or restore promptly, and in good and workmanlike manner, any building which may be constructed, damaged or destroyed thereon and to pay when due all claims for labor performed and materials furnished therefore; to comply with all laws affecting said property or requiring any alterations or improvements to be made thereon; not to commit or permit waste thereof; not to commit, suffer or permit any act upon said property in violation of law; to cultivate, irrigate, fertilize, fumigate, prune and do all other acts which, from the character or use of said property, may be reasonably necessary, the specific enumerations herein not excluding the general.

(2) To provide, maintain and deliver to Beneficiary fire insurance satisfactory to and with loss payable to Beneficiary. The amount collected under any fire or other insurance policy may be applied by Beneficiary upon any indebtedness secured hereby and in such order as Beneficiary may determine, or at option of Beneficiary the entire amount so collected or any part thereof may be released to Trustor. Such application or release shall not cure or waive any default or notice of default hereunder or invalidate any act done pursuant to such notice.

(3) To appear in and defend any action or proceeding purporting to affect the security hereof or the rights or powers of Beneficiary or Trustee; and to pay all costs and expenses, including cost of evidence of title and attorney's fees in a reasonable sum, in any such action or proceeding in which Beneficiary or Trustee may appear, and in any suit brought by Beneficiary to foreclose this Deed.

(4) To pay: at least ten days before delinquency all taxes and assessments affecting said property, including assessments, on appurtenant water stock; when due, all incumbrances, charges and liens, with interest, on said property or any part thereof, which appear to be prior or superior hereto; all costs, fees and expenses of this Trust.

Should Trustor fail to make any payment or to do any act as herein provided, then Beneficiary or Trustee, but without obligation so to do and without notice to or demand upon Trustor and without releasing Trustor from any obligation hereof, may: make or do the same in such manner and to such extent as either may deem necessary to protect the security hereof, Beneficiary or Trustee being authorized to enter upon said property for such purposes; appear in and defend any action or proceeding purporting to affect the security hereof or the rights or powers of Beneficiary or Trustee; pay, purchase, contest or compromise any incumbrance, charge or lien which in the judgment of either appears to be prior or superior hereto; and, in exercising any such powers, pay necessary expenses, employ counsel and pay his reasonable fees.

(5) To pay immediately and without demand all sums so expended by Beneficiary or Trustee, with interest from date of expenditure at the amount allowed by law in effect at the date hereof, and to pay for any statement provided for by law in effect at the date hereof, regarding the obligation secured hereby any amount demanded by the Beneficiary not to exceed the maximum allowed by law at the time when said statement is demanded.

(6) That any award of damages in connection with any condemnation for public use of or injury to said property or any part thereof is hereby assigned and shall be paid to Beneficiary who may apply or release such moneys received by him in the same manner and with the same effect as above provided for disposition of proceeds of fire or other insurance.

(7) That by accepting payment of any sum secured hereby after its due date, Beneficiary does not waive his right either to require prompt payment when due of all other sums so secured or to declare default for failure so to pay.

(8) That at any time or from time to time, without liability therefor and without notice, upon written request of Beneficiary and presentation of this Deed and said note for endorsement, and without affecting the personal liability of any person for payment of the indebtedness secured hereby, Trustee may: reconvey any part of said property; consent to the making of any map or plat thereof; join in granting any easement thereon; or join in any extension agreement or any agreement subordinating the lien or charge hereof.

(9) That upon written request of Beneficiary stating that all sums secured hereby have been paid, and upon surrender of this Deed and said note to Trustee for cancellation and retention and upon payment of its fees, Trustee shall reconvey, without warranty, the property then held hereunder. The recitals in such reconveyance of any matters or facts shall be conclusive proof of the truthfulness thereon. The grantee in such reconveyance may be described as "the person or persons legally entitled thereto." Five years after issuance of such full reconveyance, Trustee may destroy said note and this Deed (unless directed in such request to retain them).

(10) That as additional security, Trustor hereby gives to and confers upon Beneficiary the right, power and authority, during the continuance of these Trusts, to collect the rents, issues and profits of said property, reserving unto Trustor the right, prior to any default by Trustor in payment of any indebtedness secured hereby or in performance of any agreement hereunder, to collect and retain such rents, issues and profits as they become due and payable. Upon any such default, Beneficiary may at any time without notice, either in person, by agent or by a receiver to be appointed by a court, and without regard to the adequacy of any security for the indebtedness hereby secured, enter upon and take possession of said property or any part thereof, in his own name sue for or otherwise collect such rents, issues and profits, including those past due and unpaid, and apply the same, less costs and expenses of operation and collection, including reasonable attorney's fees, upon any indebtedness secured hereby, and in such order as Beneficiary may determine. The entering upon and taking possession of said property, the collection of such rents, issues and profits, and the application thereof as aforesaid, shall not cure or waive any default or notice of default hereunder or invalidate any act done pursuant to such notice.

(11) That upon default by Trustor in payment of any indebtedness secured hereby or in performance of any agreement hereunder. Beneficiary may declare all sums secured hereby immediately due and payable by delivery to Trustee of written declaration of default and demand for sale and of written notice of default and of election to cause to be sold said property, which notice Trustee shall cause to be filed for record. Beneficiary also shall deposit with Trustee this Deed, said note and all documents evidencing expenditures secured hereby.

After the lapse of such time as may then be required by law following the recordation of said notice of default, and notice of sale having been given as then required by law, Trustee, without demand on Trustor, shall sell said property at the time and place fixed by it in said notice of sale, either as a whole or in separate parcels, and in such order as it may determine, at public auction to the highest bidder for cash in lawful money of the United States, payable at time of sale. Trustee may postpone sale of all or any portion of said property by public announcement at such time and place of sale, and from time to time thereafter may postpone such sale by public announcement at the time fixed by the preceeding postponement. Trustee shall deliver to such purchaser its deed conveying the property so sold, but without any covenant or warranty, express or implied. The recitals in such deed of any matters or facts shall be conclusive proof of the truthfulness thereof. Any person, including Trustor, Trustee, or Beneficiary as hereinafter defined, may purchase at such sale.

After deducting all costs, fees and expenses of Trustee and of this Trust, including cost of evidence of title in connection with sale, Trustee shall apply the proceeds of sale to payment of: all sums expended under the terms hereof, not then repaid, with accrued interest at the amount allowed by law in effect at the date hereof; all other sums then secured hereby; and the remainder, if any, to the person or persons legally entitled thereto.

(12) Beneficiary, or any successor in ownership of any indebtedness secured hereby, may from time to time, by instrument in writing, substitute a successor or successors to any Trustee named herein or acting hereunder which instrument, executed by the Beneficiary and duly acknowledged and recorded in the office of the recorder of the county or counties where said property is situated, shall be conclusive proof of proper substitution of such successor Trustee or Trustees, who shall, without conveyance from the Trustee predecessor, succeed to all its title, estate, rights, powers and duties. Said instrument must contain the name of the original Trustor, Trustee and Beneficiary hereunder, the book and page where this Deed is recorded and the name and address of the new Trustee.

(13) That this Deed applies to, inures to the benefit of, and binds all parties hereto, their heirs, legatees, devisees, administrators, executors, successors and assigns. The term Beneficiary shall mean the owner and holder, including pledgees, of the note secured hereby, whether or not named as Beneficiary herein. In this Deed, whenever the context so requires, the masculine gender includes the feminine and/or neuter, and the singular number includes the plural.

(14) That Trustee accepts under this Trust when this Deed, duly executed and acknowledged, is made a public record as provided by law. Trustee is not obligated to notify any party hereto of pending sale under any other Deed of Trust or of any action or proceeding in which Trustor, Beneficiary or Trustee shall be a party unless brought by Trustee.

PROMISSORY NOTE SECURED BY DEED OF TRUST

1. For value received,   I individually
                                   We jointly and severally

promise to pay to the order of _____
$ _____ at _____ with interest at the rate of ___% per year:

                               from the date this note is signed until the date it is due or is paid in full, whichever date occurs last.

                               from the date this note is signed until the date it is paid in full.

2. The signer(s) of this note also agree that this note shall be paid in installments, which include principal and interest, of not less than $_____ per month, due on the first day of each month, until such time as the principal and interest are paid in full.

3. If any installment payment due under this note is not received by the holder within _____ days of its due date, the entire amount of unpaid principal shall become immediately due and payable at the option of the holder without prior notice to the signer(s) of this note.

4. In the event the holder(s) of this note prevail(s) in a lawsuit to collect on it, the signer(s) agree(s) to pay the holder(s)' attorney fees in an amount the court finds to be just and reasonable.

5. Signer(s) agree(s) that until such time as the principal and interest owed under this note are paid in full, the note shall be secured by a deed of trust to real property commonly known as _____ _____, owned by _____ executed on _____ at _____ and recorded on _____ in the records of _____ County, California.

_____   _____
Date   Date

_____   _____
Location (city or county)   Location (city or county)

_____   _____
Name of Borrower   Name of Borrower

_____   _____
Address   Address

_____   _____

_____   _____

_____   _____
Signature of Borrower   Signature of Borrower

State of California
County of _____ } ss.

On _____19__, _____, known to me or proved by satisfactory evidence to be the person(s) whose name(s) is/are subscribed above, personally appeared before me, a Notary Public for California, and acknowledged that _____ executed this note.

_____   [SEAL]
Signature of Notary

REAL ESTATE TRANSFER DISCLOSURE STATEMENT

THIS DISCLOSURE STATEMENT CONCERNS THE REAL PROPERTY SITUATED IN THE CITY OF _____, COUNTY OF _____, STATE OF CALIFORNIA, DESCRIBED AS _____ _____. THIS STATEMENT IS A DISCLOSURE OF THE CONDITION OF THE ABOVE DESCRIBED PROPERTY IN COMPLIANCE WITH SECTION 1102 OF THE CIVIL CODE AS OF _____, 19___. IT IS NOT A WARRANTY OF ANY KIND BY THE SELLER(S) OR ANY AGENT(S) REPRESENTING ANY PRINCIPAL(S) IN THIS TRANSACTION, AND IS NOT A SUBSTITUTE FOR ANY INSPECTIONS OR WARRANTIES THE PRINCIPAL(S) MAY WISH TO OBTAIN.

I
COORDINATION WITH OTHER DISCLOSURE FORMS

This Real Estate Transfer Disclosure Statement is made pursuant to Section 1102 of the Civil Code. Other statutes require disclosures, depending upon the details of the particular real estate transaction (for example: special study zone and purchase-money liens on residential property).

Substituted Disclosures: The following disclosures have or will be made in connection with this real estate transfer, and are intended to satisfy the disclosure obligations on this form, where the subject matter is the same: _____

_____
_____
_____

(list all substituted disclosure forms to be used in connection with this transaction)

II
SELLERS INFORMATION

The Seller discloses the following information with the knowledge that even though this is not a warranty, prospective Buyers may rely on this information in deciding whether and on what terms to purchase the subject property. Seller hereby authorizes any agent(s) representing any principal(s) in this transaction to provide a copy of this statement to any person or entity in connection with any actual or anticipated sale of the property.

THE FOLLOWING ARE REPRESENTATIONS MADE BY THE SELLER(S) AND ARE NOT THE REPRESENTATIONS OF THE AGENT(S), IF ANY. THIS INFORMATION IS A DISCLOSURE AND IS NOT INTENDED TO BE PART OF ANY CONTRACT BETWEEN THE BUYER AND SELLER.

Seller __is __is not occupying the property.

A. The subject property has the items checked below (read across):

__Range	__Oven	__Microwave
__Dishwasher	__Trash Compactor	__Garbage Disposal
__Washer/Dryer Hookups	__Window Screens	__Rain Gutters
__Burglar Alarms	__Smoke Detector(s)	__Fire Alarm
__T.V. Antenna	__Satellite Dish	__Intercom
__Central Heating	__Central Air Cndtng.	__Evaporator Cooler(s)
__Wall/Window Air Cndtng.	__Sprinklers	__Public Sewer System
__Septic Tank	__Sump Pump	__Water Softener
__Patio/Decking	__Built-in Barbeque	__Gazebo
__Sauna	__Pool	__Spa__Hot Tub
__Security Gate(s)	__Garage Door Opener(s)	__Number Remote Controls

Garage: __Attached __Not Attached __Carport
Pool/Spa Heater: __Gas __Solar __Electric
Water Heater: __Gas __Private Utility or
Water Supply: __City __Well
Gas Supply: __Utility __Bottled Other _____

Exhaust Fan(s) in _____ 220 Volt Wiring in _____ Fireplace(s) in _____ Gas Starter _____
Roof(s): Type: _____ Age: _____ (approx.)
Other: _____

Are there, to the best of your (Seller's) knowledge, any of the above that are not in operating condition? __Yes __No. If yes, then describe.
(Attach additional sheets if necessary.): _____

_____
_____

B. Are you (Seller) aware of any significant defects/malfunctions in any of the following? __Yes __No. If yes, check appropriate space(s) below.

__Interior Walls __Ceilings __Floors __Exterior Walls __Insulation __Roof(s) __Windows __Doors __Foundation __Slab(s) __Driveways __Sidewalks __Walls/Fences __Electrical Systems __Plumbing/Sewers/Septics __Other Structural Components (Describe: _____

_____

If any of the above is checked, explain. (Attach additional sheets if necessary): _____

_____
_____
_____

C. Are you (Seller) aware of any of the following:

1. Features of the property shared in common with adjoining landowners, such as walls, fences, and driveways, whose use or responsibility for maintenance may have an effect on the subject property .... __Yes __No

2. Any encroachments, easements or similar matters that may affect your interest in the subject property .... __Yes __No

3. Room additions, structural modifications, or other alterations or repairs made without necessary permits . . . . __Yes __No
4. Room additions, structural modifications, or other alterations or repairs not in compliance with building codes . . . . __Yes __No
5. Landfill (compacted or otherwise) on the property or any portion thereof . . . . __Yes __No
6. Any settling from any cause, or slippage, sliding, or other soil problems . . . . . . __Yes __No
7. Flooding, drainage or grading problems . . . . __Yes __No
8. Major damage to the property or any of the structures from fire, earthquake, floods, or landslides . . . . __Yes __No
9. Any zoning violations, nonconforming uses, violations of "setback" requirements . . . . __Yes __No
10. Neighborhood noise problems or other nuisances . . . . __Yes __No
11. CC&R's or other deed restrictions or obligations . . . . __Yes __No
12. Homeowners' Association which has any authority over the subject property . . . . __Yes __No
13. Any "common area" (facilities such as pools, tennis courts, walkways, or other areas co-owned in undivided interest with others) . . . . __Yes __No
14. Any notices of abatement or citations against the property . . . . __Yes __No
15. Any lawsuits against the seller threatening to or affecting this real property . . . . __Yes __No

If the answer to any of these is yes, explain. (Attach additional sheets if necessary.): _____
_____
_____
_____

Seller certifies that the information herein is true and correct to the best of the Seller's knowledge as of the date signed by the Seller.

Seller _____
Date _____
Seller _____
Date _____

III
AGENTS INSPECTION DISCLOSURE
(Please Print)

IV
AGENTS INSPECTION DISCLOSURE
(To be completed only if the agent who has obtained the offer is other than the agent above.)

THE UNDERSIGNED, BASED ON A REASONABLY COMPETENT AND DILIGENT VISUAL INSPECTION OF THE ACCESSIBLE AREAS OF THE PROPERTY, STATES THE FOLLOWING:

(Please Print)

V

BUYER(S) AND SELLER(S) MAY WISH TO OBTAIN PROFESSIONAL ADVICE AND/OR INSPECTIONS OF THE PROPERTY AND TO PROVIDE FOR APPROPRIATE PROVISIONS IN A CONTRACT BETWEEN BUYER AND SELLER(S) WITH RESPECT TO ANY ADVICE/INSPECTIONS/DEFECTS.

(To be completed only if the seller is represented by an agent in this transaction.)

THE UNDERSIGNED, BASED ON THE ABOVE INQUIRY OF THE SELLER(S) AS TO THE CONDITION OF THE PROPERTY AND BASED ON A REASONABLY COMPETENT AND DILIGENT

VISUAL INSPECTION OF THE ACCESSIBLE AREAS OF THE PROPERTY IN CONJUNCTION WITH THAT INQUIRY, STATES THE FOLLOWING: _____
_____
_____
_____

Agent (Broker
Representing Seller) _____ By _____ Date
_____
(Associate Licensee or Broker-Signature)

_____
_____
_____
_____

Agent (Broker
obtaining the Offer) _____ By _____ Date
_____
(Associate Licensee or Broker-Signature)

I/WE ACKNOWLEDGE RECEIPT OF A COPY OF THIS STATEMENT.

Seller _____ Date _____ Buyer
_____ Date _____
Seller _____ Date _____ Buyer
_____ Date _____

Agent (Broker
Representing Seller) _____ By _____ Date
_____
(Associate Licensee or Broker-Signature)

Agent (Broker
obtaining the Offer) _____ By _____ Date
_____
(Associate Licensee or Broker-Signature)

A REAL ESTATE BROKER IS QUALIFIED TO ADVISE ON REAL ESTATE. IF YOU DESIRE LEGAL ADVICE, CONSULT YOUR ATTORNEY.

SPECIAL STUDIES ZONE DISCLOSURE

The real property at _____,

_____ County, California, lies within a special studies zone

designated by the California Department of Geology.

This disclosure is made under California Public Resources Code Section 2621.9.

_____   _____, 19_____
Transferor

I acknowledge that I have received a copy of this disclosure form.

_____   _____, 19_____
Transferee

FORM FOR ACKNOWLEDGMENT: MILITARY PERSONNEL

On this the _____ day of _____, 19___, before me,

_____, the undersigned officer, personally appeared

_____, known to me (or satisfactorily proven) to be (a)

serving in the armed forces of the United States, (b) a spouse of a person serving in the

armed forces of the United States, or (c) a person serving with, employed by, or

accompanying the armed forces of the United States outside the United States and

outside the Canal Zone, Puerto Rico, Guam, and the Virgin Islands, and to be the person

whose name is subscribed to the within instrument and acknowledged that he executed

the same. And the undersigned does further certify that he is at the date of this

certificate a commissioned officer in the active service of the armed forces of the

United States having the general powers of a notary public under the provisions of

Section 936 of Title 10 of the United States Code (Public Law 90-632).

_____

_____

Signature of officer and serial number, rank,
branch of service and capacity in which signed.

Declaration of Exemption from Documentary Transfer Tax: Gift of Real Property

Grantor has not received and will not receive consideration from grantee for the transfer made by the attached deed. Therefore, under Revenue and Taxation Code Sec. 11911, the deed is not subject to the Documentary Transfer Tax.

I declare under penalty of perjury under the laws of California that the foregoing is true and correct.

_____

Grantor

Date:_____   _____, California

_____

Grantor

Date:_____   _____, California

DECLARATION OF EXEMPTION FROM DOCUMENTARY TRANSFER TAX: DIVISION OF MARITAL REAL PROPERTY

The transfer made by the attached deed is made for the purpose of dividing community, quasi-community or quasi-marital real property between spouses, as required by:

☐ a judgment decreeing a dissolution of the marriage or legal separation, by a judgment of nullity, or by any other judgment or order rendered pursuant to Part 5 of Division 4 of the Civil Code, or

☐ a written agreement between the spouses executed in contemplation of such a judgment or order.

Therefore, under Revenue and Taxation Code Sec. 11927, the deed is not subject to the Documentary Transfer Tax.

I declare under penalty of perjury under the laws of California that the foregoing is true and correct.

_____

Grantor

Date:_____   _____, California

_____

Grantor

Date:_____   _____, California

INDEX

Business and Finance

How To Form Your Own Corporation
By attorney Mancuso. Provides all the forms, Bylaws, Articles, minutes of meeting, stock certificates and instructions necessary to form your small profit corporation. Includes a thorough discussion of the practical and legal aspects of incorporation, including the tax consequences.

California Edition	$24.95
Texas Edition	$21.95
New York Edition	$19.95
Florida Edition	$19.95

The Non-Profit Corporation Handbook
By attorney Mancuso. Includes all the forms, Bylaws, Articles, minutes, and instructions you need to form a non-profit corporation. Step-by-step instructions on how to choose a name, draft Articles and Bylaws, attain favorable tax status. Thorough information on federal tax exemptions, which groups outside of California will find particularly useful.
California only $24.95

The California Professional Corporation Handbook
By attorneys Mancuso and Honigsberg. In California a number of professions must fulfill special requirements when forming a corporation. Among them are lawyers, dentists, doctors and other health professionals, accountants and certain social workers. This book contains detailed information on the special requirements of every profession and all the forms and instructions necessary to form a professional corporation.
California only $29.95

Marketing Without Advertising
By Phillips and Rasberry. A creative and practical guide that shows small businesspersons how to avoid wasting money on advertising. The authors, experienced business consultants, show how to implement an ongoing marketing plan to tell potential and current customers that yours is a quality business worth trusting, recommending and coming back to.
National Edition $14.00

Billpayers' Rights
By attorney Warner. Complete information on bankruptcy, student loans, wage attachments, dealing with bill collectors and collection agencies, credit cards, car repossessions, homesteads, child support and much more.
California only $12.95

Chapter 13: The Federal Plan to Repay Your Debts
By attorney Kosel. This book allows an individual to develop and carry out a feasible plan to pay most of his/her debts over a three-year period. Chapter 13 is an alternative to straight bankruptcy and yet it still means the end of creditor harassment, wage attachments and other collection efforts. Comes complete with all necessary forms and worksheets.
National Edition $14.95

The Partnership Book
By attorneys Clifford and Warner. When two or more people join to start a small business, one of the most basic needs is to establish a solid, legal partnership agreement. This book supplies a number of sample agreements which you can use as is. Buy-out clauses, unequal sharing of assets, and limited partnerships are all discussed in detail.
National Edition $18.95

Bankruptcy: Do-It-Yourself
By attorney Kosel. Tells you exactly what bankruptcy is all about and how it affects your credit rating, property and debts, with complete details on property you can keep under the state and federal exempt property rules. Shows you step-by-step how to do it yourself; comes with all necessary forms and instructions.
National Edition $15.95

Small Time Operator
By Kamoroff, C.P.A.. Shows you how to start and operate your small business, keep your books, pay your taxes and stay out of trouble. Comes complete with a year's supply of ledgers and worksheets designed especially for small businesses, and contains invaluable information on permits, licenses, financing, loans, insurance, bank accounts, etc. Published by Bell Springs.
National Edition $10.95

Start-Up Money: How to Finance Your Small Business
By McKeever. For anyone about to start a business or revamp an existing one, this book shows how to write a business plan, draft a loan package and find sources of small business finance.
National Edition $12.95

The Independent Paralegal's Handbook: How to Provide Legal Services Without Going to Jail
By attorney Warner. More and more nonlawyers are opening legal typing services to help people prepare their own papers for divorce, bankruptcy, incorporation, eviction, etc. Called independent paralegals, these legal pioneers pose much the same challenge to the legal establishment as midwives do to conventional medicine. Written by Nolo Press co-founder Ralph Warner, who established one of the first divorce typing services in 1973, this controversial book is sure to become the bible of the new movement aimed at delivering routine legal services to the public at a reasonable price.
National Edition $12.95

Estate Planning, Wills & Probate

Plan Your Estate: Wills, Probate Avoidance, Trusts and Taxes
By attorney Clifford. Comprehensive information on making a will, alternatives to probate, planning to limit inheritance and estate taxes, living trusts, and providing for family and friends. Explains new California statutory will and includes actual forms.
California Edition $15.95

Nolo's Simple Will Book
By attorney Clifford. This book will show you how to draft a will without a lawyer in any state except Louisiana. Covers all the basics, including what to do about children, whom you can designate to carry out your wishes, and how to comply with the technical legal requirements of each state. Includes examples and many alternative clauses from which to choose.
National Edition $14.95

WillWriter—a software/book package
By Legisoft. Use your computer to prepare and update your own valid will. A manual provides help in areas such as tax planning and probate avoidance. Runs on Apple II+, IIe, IIc, the Mac, Commodore and the IBM PC (and most PC compatibles).
National Edition $49.95

How to Settle A Simple Estate
By Nissley. Forms and instructions necessary to settle a California resident's estate after death. This book deals with joint tenancy and community property transfers as well as showing you how to actually probate an estate, step-by-step. The book is aimed at the executor, administrator or family member who will have the actual responsibility to settle the estate.
California Edition $19.95

Family and Friends

How to Do Your Own Divorce
By attorney Sherman. This is the original "do-your-own-law" book. It contains tearout copies of all the court forms required for an uncontested dissolution, as well as instructions for certain special forms.
California Edition $14.95
Texas Edition $12.95

A Legal Guide for Lesbian/Gay Couples
By attorneys Curry and Clifford. Here is a book that deals specifically with legal matters of lesbian and gay couples: raising children (custody, support, living with a lover), buying property together, wills, etc. and comes complete with sample contracts and agreements.
National Edition $17.95

The Living Together Kit
By attorneys Ihara and Warner. A legal guide for unmarried couples with information about buying or sharing property, the Marvin decision, paternity statements, medical emergencies and tax consequences. Contains a sample will and Living Together Contract.
National Edition $14.95

California Marriage and Divorce Law
By attorneys Ihara and Warner. This book contains invaluable information for married couples and those considering marriage or remarriage on community and separate property, names, debts, children, buying a house, etc. Includes prenuptial contracts, a simple will, probate avoidance information and an explanation of gift and inheritance taxes. Discusses "secret marriage" and "common law" marriage.
California only $14.95

Social Security, Medicare & Pensions: The Sourcebook for Older Americans
By attorney Matthews. The most comprehensive resource tool on the income, rights and benefits of Americans over 55. Includes detailed information on social security, retirement rights, Medicare, Medicaid, supplemental security income, private pensions, age discrimination, as well as a thorough explanation of the new social security legislation.
National Edition $14.95

How to Modify & Collect Child Support in California
By attorneys Matthews, Segal and Willis. California court awards for child support have radically increased in the last two years. This book contains the forms and instructions to obtain the benefits of this change without a lawyer and collect support directly from a person's wages or benefits, if necessary.
California only $17.95

How to Adopt Your Stepchild
By Zagone. Shows you how to prepare all the legal forms; includes information on how to get the consent of the natural parent and how to conduct an "abandonment" proceeding. Discusses appearing in court and making changes in birth certificates.
California only $17.95

The Power of Attorney Book
By attorney Clifford. Covers the process which allows you to arrange for someone else to protect your rights and property should you become incapable of doing so. Discusses the advantages and drawbacks and gives complete instructions for establishing a power of attorney yourself.
National Edition $15.95

How to Change Your Name
By attorneys Loeb and Brown. Changing one's name is a very simple procedure. Using this book, you can file the necessary papers yourself, saving $200 to $300 in attorney's fees. Comes complete with all forms and instructions for the court petition method or ths simpler usage method.
California only $14.95

Your Family Records: How to Preserve Personal, Financial and Legal History
By Pladsen and attorney Clifford. Helps you organize and record all sorts of items that will affect you and your family when death or disability occur, e.g., where to find your will and deed to the house. Includes information about probate avoidance, joint ownership of property and genealogical research. Space is provided for financial and legal records.
National Edition $14.95

Landlord/Tenant

Tenants' Rights
By attorneys Moskovitz, Warner and Sherman. Discusses everything tenants need to know in order to protect themselves: getting deposits returned, breaking a lease, getting repairs made, using Small Claims Court, dealing with an unscrupulous landlord, forming a tenants' organization, etc. Sample Fair-to-Tenants lease, rental agreements, and unlawful detainer answer forms.
California Edition $14.95

The Landlord's Law Book: Rights and Responsibilities
By attorney Brown. Now, for the first time, there is an accessible, easy to understand law book written specifically for landlords. Covers the areas of discrimination, insurance, tenants' privacy, leases, security deposits, rent control, liability, and rent with-holding.
California only $19.95

The Landlord's Law Book: Evictions
By attorneys Brown and Warner. This is the most comprehensive manual available on how to do each step of an eviction, and the only one to deal with rent control cities and contested evictions including how to represent yourself in court if necessary. All the required forms, with directions on how to complete and file them, are included. Vol. 1 covers Rights and Responsibilities.
California only $19.95

Landlording
By Robinson (Express Press). Written for the conscientious landlord or landlady, this comprehensive guide discusses maintenance and repairs, getting good tenants, how to avoid evictions, record keeping and taxes.
National Edition $17.95

Real Estate

All About Escrow
(Express Press) By Gadow. This book gives you a good understanding of what your escrow officer should be doing for you. Includes advice about inspections, financing, condominiums and cooperatives.
National Edition $12.95

The Deeds Book
By attorney Randolph. Adding or removing a name from a deed, giving up interest in community property at divorce, putting a house in joint tenancy to avoid probate, all these transactions require a change in the way title to real estate is held. This book shows you how to choose the right deed, fill it out and record it.
California Edition $15.95

Homebuyers: Lambs to the Slaughter
By attorney Bashinsky (Menasha Ridge Press). Written by a lawyer/broker, this book describes how sellers, agents, lenders and lawyers are out to fleece you, the buyer, and advises how to protect your interests.
National Edition $12.95

For Sale By Owner
By Devine. The average California home sold for $130,000 in 1986. That meant the average seller paid $7800 in broker's commissions. This book will show you how to sell your own home and save the money. All the background information and legal technicalities are included to help you do the job yourself and with confidence.
California Edition $24.95

Homestead Your House
By attorney Warner. Under the California Homestead Act, you can file a Declaration of Homestead and thus protect your home from being sold to satisfy most debts. This book explains this simple and inexpensive procedure and includes all the forms and instructions. Contains information on exemptions for mobile homes and houseboats.
California only $8.95

Copyrights & Patents

Legal Care for Your Software
By attorney Remer. Shows the software programmer how to protect his/her work through the use of trade secret, trademark, copyright, patent and, most especially, contractual laws and agreements. This book is full of forms and instructions that give programmers the hands-on information they need.
International Edition $24.95

Intellectual Property Law Dictionary
By attorney Elias. "Intellectual Property" includes ideas, creations and inventions. The Dictionary is designed for inventors, authors, programmers, journalists, scientists and business people who must understand how the law affects the ownership and control of new ideas and technologies. Divided into sections on: Trade Secrets, Copyrights, Trademarks, Patents and Contracts. More than a dictionary, it places terms in context as well as defines them.
National Edition $17.95

How to Copyright Software
By attorney Salone. Shows the serious programmer or software developer how to protect his or her programs through the legal device of copyright.
International Edition $24.95

Patent It Yourself
By attorney Pressman. Complete instructions on how to do a patent search and file for a patent in the U.S. Also covers how to choose the appropriate form of protection (copyright, trademark, trade secret, etc.), how to evaluate salability of inventions, patent prosecution, marketing, use of the patent, foreign filing, licensing, etc. Tearout forms are included
National Edition $24.95

Researching the Law

California Civil Code
(West Publishing) Statutes covering a wide variety of topics, rights and duties in the landlord/tenant relationship, marriage and divorce, contracts, transfers of real estate, consumer credit, power of attorney, and trusts.
California only $17.00

California Code of Civil Procedure

(West Publishing) Statutes governing most judicial and administrative procedures: unlawful detainer (eviction) proceedings, small claims actions, homestead procedures, wage garnishments, recording of liens, statutes of limitation, court procedures, arbitration, and appeals.
California only $17.00

Legal Research: How to Find and Understand the Law

By attorney Elias. A hands-on guide to unraveling the mysteries of the law library. For paralegals, law students, consumer activists, legal secretaries, business and media people. Shows exactly how to find laws relating to specific cases or legal questions, interpret statutes and regulations, find and research cases, understand case citations and Shepardize them.
National Edition $14.95

Rules and Tools

Make Your Own Contract

By attorney Elias. Provides tear-out contracts, with instructions, for non-commercial use. Covers lending money, selling or leasing personal property (e.g., cars, boats), leasing and storing items (with friends, neighbors), doing home repairs, and making deposits to hold personal property pending final payment. Includes an appendix listing all the contracts found in Nolo books.
National Edition $12.95

The People's Law Review

Edited by Warner. This is the first compendium of people's law resources ever published. Contains articles on mediation and the new "non-adversary" mediation centers, information on selfhelp law programs and centers (for tenants, artists, battered women, the disabled, etc.); and articles dealing with many common legal problems which show people how to do-it-themselves.
National Edition $8.95

The Criminal Records Book

By attorney Siegel. Takes you step-by-step through the procedures available to get your records sealed, destroyed or changed. Detailed discussion on your criminal record what it is, how it can harm you, how to correct inaccuracies, marijuana possession records and juvenile court records.
California only $14.95

Everybody's Guide to Small Claims Court

By attorney Warner. Guides you step-by-step through the Small Claims procedure, providing practical information on how to evaluate your case, file and serve papers, prepare and present your case, and, most important, how to collect when you win. Separate chapters focus on common situations (landlord-tenant, automobile sales and repair, etc.).
National Edition $10.95
California Edition $14.95

Fight Your Ticket

By attorney Brown. A comprehensive manual on how to fight your traffic ticket. Radar, drunk driving, preparing for court, arguing your case to a judge, cross-examining witnesses are all covered.
California only $14.95

How to Become a United States Citizen

By Sally Abel. Detailed explanation of the naturalization process. Includes step-by-step instructions from filing for naturalization to the final oath of allegiance. Includes a study guide on U.S. history and government. Text is written in both English and Spanish.
National Edition $9.95

Draft, Registration and The Law

How it works, what to do, advice and strategies.
California only $9.95

Murder on the Air

By Ralph Warner and Toni Ihara. An unconventional murder mystery set in Berkeley, California. When a noted environmentalist and anti-nuclear activist is killed at a local radio station, the Berkeley violent crime squad swings into action. James Rivers, an unplugged lawyer, and Sara Tamura, Berkeley's first female murder squad detective, lead the chase. The action is fast, furious and fun. $5.95

29 Reasons Not to Go to Law School

A humorous and irreverent look at the dubious pleasures of going to law school. By attorneys Ihara and Warner, with contributions by fellow lawyers and illustrations by Mari Stein. $6.95

Order Form

Quantity	Title	Unit Price	Total

Prices subject to change

___Please send me a catalogue

Tax: (CA only; San Mateo, LA, & Bart Counties, 6 1/2%, Santa Clara 7%, all others, 6%)

Subtotal_____

Tax_____

Postage & Handling_____

Total_____

Postage & Handling:

No. of Books	Postage & Handling
1	$1.50
2-3	$2.00
4-5	$2.50

Over 5, add 5% of total before tax

Please allow 3-5 weeks for delivery. For faster service, add $1 for UPS delivery (no P.O. boxes, please).

Name_____

Address_____

_____

_____VISA   _____Mastercard

#_____ exp._____

Signature_____

Phone (   )_____

ORDERS: Credit card information or a check may be sent to NOLO Press, 950 Parker St., Berkeley,CA 94710

Use your credit card and call our **800 lines** for for faster service:

Orders only: **US: 800-992-NOLO**
CA: 800-445-NOLO
(M-F, 9:00 - 5:00 PDT)

For general information call (415)549-1976

or

Send a check only to NOLO Distributing, Box Box 544, Occidental, CA 955465